JN025783

英文精読教室

第1巻

物語を楽しむ

柴田元幸 編・訳・註

研究社

英文精読教室
第1巻
物語を楽しむ

PRINTED IN JAPAN

はじめに

この「英文精読教室」は、読者が英語の小説を原文で読むのを助けるためのシリーズです。

まずは編者がこれまで読んだり訳したりしてきたなかで、とりわけ面白いと思った短篇小説を選び、6巻それぞれ、ひとつのテーマに沿って作品を並べてあります。第1巻から順に読む必要はありません。ご自分が惹かれるテーマから手にとっていただければと思います。各巻、まずはウォームアップ的にごく短い作品を据えたあとは、時代順に並んでいますが、これも順番に読む必要はありません。各作品の難易度を1～3で示してありますから（1が一番易しい）、読む際の目安にしてください。

どの作品にも詳しい註を施しました。註というものはつねに諸刃の剣であり、読者によって「小さな親切」にも「大きなお世話」にもなりえますが、このシリーズではどちらかというと、一部の読者には「大きなお世話」になる危険も覚悟で、やや多めに註が施してあります。ご自分の読みが妥当かどうかを確認してもらえるよう、右側のページには対訳を盛り込みました。少し語学的に敷居が高い、と思える作品に関しては、まず対訳を読んでもらってから原文に向かう、というやり方もあると思います。

「まっとうな翻訳があるなら、何も原文で読む必要はないじゃないか」とおっしゃる読者もいらっしゃるでしょう。むしろその方が多数派かもしれません。僕自身、まっとうな翻訳を作ることを、長年主たる仕事にしてきましたから、そういう読者が大勢いてくださるのはとても嬉しいことです。

その反面、原文で読むことの楽しさを味わいたい、と思われる読者も一定数おられるという確信も僕にはあります。そのなかで、何の助けもなしに辞書だけで原書を読むのはちょっと厳しい、という読者がまた一定数おられるという確信もまたあります。

かつては近所の書店に行けば、註釈つきの英語読本や英和対訳本が並んでいて、僕も中学のころから日本のおとぎ話やO・ヘンリーの短篇などを易しい英語で書き直した本を買ってノートに訳文を書いて楽しんだものですが、ふと気がつくとそういう本もずいぶん減ってしまいました。この残念な欠如を、本シリーズが少しでも是正できれば幸いです。

編訳註者

英文精読教室
第1巻
物語を楽しむ

目次

Ending for a Ghost Story

I. A. Ireland

幽霊ばなしのためのエンディング

I・A・アイルランド

難易度 1

★☆☆

I・A・アイルランド
(I. A. Ireland, 1871? - ?)

アルゼンチンの大作家ホルヘ・ルイス・ボルヘスが A・ビオイ＝カサーレス、シルビーナ・オカンポと作った幻想小説アンソロジー *Antología de la literatura fantástica*（1940）の中に、この “Ending for a Ghost Story” が掲載されている（スペイン語版のタイトルは “Final para un cuento fantástico”）。そこに付された解説によれば、I・A・アイルランドは 1871 年スタッフォードシャー北部の町ハンリーに生まれた学者で、シェークスピアに原稿を遺贈された人物を祖先として捏造したペテン師ウィリアム・H・アイルランド（1775-1835）の子孫を自称していた。

'How ❶eerie!' said the girl, ❷advancing cautiously. 'And what a heavy door!' She touched it as she spoke and it suddenly ❸swung to with ❹a click.

'❺Good Lord!' said the man, '❻I don't believe there's a handle inside. ❼Why, you've locked us both in!'

'Not both of us. Only one of us,' said the girl, and before his eyes she ❽passed straight through the door, and ❾vanished.

❶ eerie: 気味が悪い
❷ advancing cautiously: 慎重に進んで
❸ swung to <swing to:（ドアなどが）さっと閉じる（to は前置詞でなく副詞）
❹ a click: かちりという音
❺ Good Lord: 大変だ、なんてこった
❻ I don't believe: I don't think
❼ Why: 驚き・承認・抗議・戸惑い等々、実にいろんな感情を伝えうる言葉。ここでは、閉じ込められてしまった男が愕然としている思いを伝えている。
❽ passed straight through ...: ～をまっすぐ通り抜けた
❾ vanish(ed): 消える

「なんて気味悪いんでしょう！」と娘は、そろそろと進みながら言った。「それになんて重い扉！」。そう言いながら彼女が触れると、扉はいきなり動いてかちっと閉まった。

「なんてこった！」と男は言った。「この扉、こっち側には把手がないぞ。僕たち、二人とも閉じ込められてしまったよ！」

「二人ともじゃないわ。一人だけよ」と娘は言って、男の目の前で、扉をすうっと抜けて、消えた。

ちなみに

ボルヘスらのアンソロジーの解説をさらに引けば、I・A・アイルランドの著書には『悪夢小史』(*A Brief History of Nightmares*, 1899)、『スペイン文学』(*Spanish Literature*, 1911)、『新訳タキトゥス年代記第10巻』(*The Tenth Book of Annals of Tacitus, newly done into English*, 1911) があるという。またこの「幽霊ばなしのためのエンディング」は *Visitations* (1919) から取った、とある。しかし、世界の主要図書館のカタログを見ても、これらの本に関する情報はいっさい出てこない。

The Monkey's Paw

W. W. Jacobs

猿の手

W・W・ジェイコブズ

W・W・ジェイコブズ
(William Wymark Jacobs, 1863-1943)

イギリスの作家。ユーモア作家としてデビューし、1880 年代から 1930 年代にかけて 300 本以上の作品を発表して大きな人気を誇ったが、現在ではもっぱら一本の短篇、この 'The Monkey's Paw' によって記憶されている。しかし 'The Monkey's Paw' は誰もが怪奇小説の古典と認める傑作であり、これまで何度も何度も舞台化・映画化・ドラマ化されている。

I.

❶Without, the night was cold and wet, but in the small ❷parlour of Laburnam Villa the blinds were drawn and the fire burned brightly. Father and son were at chess, the former, who ❸possessed ideas about the game involving radical changes, putting his king into such ❹sharp and unnecessary perils that it even❺provoked comment from the white-haired old lady knitting ❻placidly by the fire.

'❼Hark at the wind,' said Mr. White, who, having seen a fatal mistake after it was too late, ❽was amiably desirous of preventing his son from seeing it.

'I'm listening,' said the latter, ❾grimly surveying the board as he stretched out his hand. '❿Check.'

'⓫I should hardly think that he'd come ⓬to-night,' said his father, with his hand ⓭poised over the board.

❶ Without: 外では。現代では Outside が普通。
❷ (a) parlour: 居間
❸ possessed ideas about the game involving radical changes: （チェスという）ゲームに関する、根本的な変化を伴うアイデアを持っていた。自分では何か独自の必勝法のようなものを父親が持っているつもりでいる、ということをユーモラスに言っている。
❹ sharp and unnecessary perils: 大きな、不要な危険
❺ provoke(d): ～を引き起こす、誘発する
❻ placidly: 穏やかに
❼ Hark at the wind: 「風の音を聞け」。現代では Listen to the wind が普通。
❽ was amiably desirous of preventing his son from seeing it: 直訳すれば「息子がそれ（その致命的な間違い）を見てとるのを妨げることを、愛想よく望

I.

外は寒い夜で、雨も降っていたが、ラバーナム荘の小さな居間ではブラインドが下ろされ、暖炉はあかあかと燃えていた。父と息子がチェスをしていて、父の方はチェスというゲームをめぐって根本的な変革を伴う見解を有しているせいで、キングを甚大かつ不要な危険に陥れたため、暖炉のそばで静かに編み物をしていた白髪の老婦人までが口をはさむことになった。

「風の音を聴いてごらん」とホワイト氏は、致命的な過ちに気がついたものの時すでに遅く、息子が気づくのを邪魔しようと愛想よく言ってみた。

「聴いてますよ」と息子の方は、厳(いか)めしい顔で盤面を見渡しながら片手をつき出した。「王手(チェック)」

「今夜はもうあの男、来そうにないな」と父親が、片手を盤の上に浮かせて言う。

「詰み(メイト)」と息子が答えた。

「町外れの暮らしはこれだから嫌だ」とホワイト氏が出し抜けにすごい剣幕

んでいた」。

❾ grimly surveying the board: チェス盤を厳(いか)めしく見わたして

❿ Check: 王手

⓫ I should hardly think that ...: まず〜ということはないだろう

⓬ to-night: 20 世紀初頭くらいまでは to-day や to-night といった書き方も一般的だった。

⓭ poise(d): (宙に) 保つ

'❶Mate,' replied the son.

'❷That's the worst of living so far out,' ❸bawled Mr. White, ❹with sudden and unlooked-for violence; '❺of all the beastly, slushy, out-of-the-way places to live in, this is the worst. ❻Pathway's ❼a bog, and the road's ❽a torrent. I don't know what people are thinking about. I suppose because only two houses in the road ❾are let, they think it doesn't matter.'

'Never mind, dear,' said his wife, ❿soothingly; 'perhaps you'll win the next one.'

Mr. White ⓫looked up sharply, ⓬just in time to intercept a knowing glance between mother and son. ⓭The words died away on his lips, and he hid a guilty grin in his thin grey beard.

'There he is,' said Herbert White, as the gate ⓮banged to loudly and heavy footsteps came toward the door.

The old man rose ⓯with hospitable haste, and opening the door, was heard ⓰condoling with the new arrival. The new arrival also

❶ Mate: 詰み
❷ That's the worst of living so far out:（町から）遠く離れた暮らしはこれが最悪だ
❸ bawl(ed): 叫ぶ、わめく。何か不満があって叫ぶ感じ。
❹ with sudden and unlooked-for violence: 突然の、思いがけない剣幕で
❺ of all the beastly, slushy, out-of-the-way places:（数ある）ひどい、ぬかるんだ、辺鄙な場所のなかで
❻ Pathway('s): 道路から家までの私道のこと。
❼ a bog: 沼
❽ a torrent: 急流
❾ are let: 貸家になっている
❿ soothingly: 慰めるように、なだめるように

で声を張り上げた。「住めたもんじゃない泥んこの山里も数あるが、ここは最悪だ。家の前は沼同然、道路は川。いったいみんな何を考えているのかね。きっと、道路沿いで貸家は二軒しかないところなぞどうでもいいと思ってるんだろうよ」

「いいじゃないの、あなた」と妻がなだめるように言った。「次は勝てるかもしれないわよ」

ホワイト氏はきっと顔を上げ、母と子が訳知り顔の視線を交わそうとするのを間一髪捕らえた。氏の唇に浮かんだ言葉が消え去り、薄い灰色のあごひげのなかにバツの悪そうな苦笑いが隠れた。

「来ましたよ」とハーバート・ホワイトが、表の木戸が大きな音を立てて閉まり重い足音が玄関に近づいてくるのを聞いて言った。

老人は客を迎えにいそいそと立ち上がった。彼がドアを開けて、着いた人間を相手に、あいにくの天気だねえ難儀したでしょう、と言っているのが聞こえた。着いた方も、ええたしかに難儀いたしまして、などと言っているも

⓫ looked up sharply: さっと顔を上げた
⓬ just in time to intercept a knowing glance: 訳知り顔のまなざしを、間一髪のタイミングで捕らえて
⓭ The words died away on his lips: 言葉は唇に浮かんだものの消えていった
⓮ banged to: ばたんと閉まった。この to は *The wind blew the door to.*（風でドアが閉まった）などと同じ。p. 8, 註❸にも出てきた。
⓯ with hospitable haste: 直訳は「もてなしのよい急ぎ方で」。日本語で言う「いそいそと」に近いか。
⓰ condoling with the new arrival: 着いたばかりの人相手に同情の言葉を言って。おそらく「雨の中よく来てくれたねえ」などと言っている。

condoled with himself, so that Mrs. White said, '❶Tut, tut!' and coughed gently as her husband entered the room, followed by a tall, ❷burly man, ❸beady of eye and ❹rubicund of ❺visage.

'❻Sergeant-Major Morris,' he said, introducing him.

The sergeant-major shook hands, and taking the ❼proffered seat by the fire, watched ❽contentedly while his host got out whiskey and tumblers and ❾stood a small copper kettle on the fire.

At the third glass his eyes got brighter, and he began to talk, the little family circle ❿regarding with eager interest this visitor ⓫from distant parts, as he ⓬squared his broad shoulders in the chair and spoke of wild scenes and ⓭doughty deeds; of wars and ⓮plagues and ⓯strange peoples.

'Twenty-one years of it,' said Mr. White, nodding at his wife and son. 'When he went away ⓰he was a slip of a youth in the warehouse. Now look at him.'

'⓱He don't look to have taken much harm,' said Mrs. White,

❶ Tut, tut!: じれったさを伝える音。通例このように二度言う。
❷ burly: たくましい、頑丈な
❸ beady: (ビーズのように) 小さくて丸い
❹ rubicund: 赤い、血色のよい
❺ (a) visage: 顔、顔つき
❻ Sergeant-Major: (英陸軍の) 特務曹長
❼ proffer(ed): ～を差し出す、薦める
❽ contentedly: 満足げに
❾ stood a small copper kettle on the fire: 小さな銅の薬罐を火にかけた。stood は現代なら put が普通。
❿ regarding with eager interest ...: ～を興味津々眺めて
⓫ from distant parts: 遠い地域から来た

のだから、ホワイト夫人はじれったそうに舌打ちし、軽く咳払いをした。と、夫が戻ってきて、それに続いて、背の高いがっしりした、目は小さく丸く赤ら顔の男が入ってきた。

「モリス特務曹長だ」と夫は客を紹介した。

特務曹長は皆と握手し、勧められるまま暖炉ぎわの席に腰掛け、家のあるじがウイスキーとタンブラーを出してきて小さな銅の薬罐を火にかけるのを心地よさそうに眺めていた。

三杯目になると客の目もだんだん輝いてきて、遠方からの訪問者を小さな家族の輪が興味津々見守るなか、男はぽつぽつと話をはじめた。幅広の肩を椅子に押し込んで、奇怪な情景や獰猛な行為を語り、戦争や疫病や不思議な民族を語った。

「二十一年になる」とホワイト氏は言って、妻と息子に向かってうなずいた。「出ていったときはほんのヒヨッ子だったよ。それがいまはどうだ」

「立派に生き抜いてこられたようね」とホワイト夫人が如才なく言った。

⓬ squared his broad shoulders in the chair: 広い両肩を椅子に押し込んだ

⓭ doughty deeds: 勇敢な行ない

⓮ plague(s): 疫病

⓯ strange peoples: いくつもの奇妙な民族。people は「民族」の意味では a people, two peoples ... というふうに s の付く名詞となる。

⓰ he was a slip of a youth in the warehouse: 直訳は「倉庫にいるちっぽけな若者」。a slip of a youth (boy, girl など) は古風なイディオムで、痩せた小さな人間を言う。in the warehouse は不明だが、まだ世の表舞台に出ていないということか。

⓱ He don't look to have taken much harm: 直訳は「大した害は受けていないように見える」。立派に生きてきたようね、ということ。He doesn't ではなく He don't になっている（教養ある人間はしない言い方）のが庶民的に響く。

politely.

'I'd like to go to India myself,' said the old man, '❶just to look round a bit, you know.'

'❷Better where you are,' said the sergeant-major, shaking his head. He put down the empty glass, and sighing softly, shook it again.

'I should like to see those old temples and ❸fakirs and jugglers,' said the old man. '❹What was that you started telling me the other day about a monkey's paw or something, Morris?'

'Nothing,' said the soldier, hastily. '❺Leastways nothing worth hearing.'

'Monkey's paw?' said Mrs. White, curiously.

'Well, ❻it's just a bit of what you might call magic, perhaps,' said the sergeant-major, ❼offhandedly.

His three listeners ❽leaned forward eagerly. The visitor ❾absent-mindedly put his empty glass to his lips and then set it

❶ just to look round a bit: まあちょっと見て回るために
❷ Better where you are: You're better off where you are; You'd better stay where you are
❸ fakirs and jugglers: 托鉢僧や曲芸師
❹ What was that you started telling me the other day about a monkey's paw or something: 直訳は「先日君が猿の手だか何だかについて話しはじめた、あれは何だったのか」。動物の、かぎつめのある「手」は hand と言わずに paw と言う。
❺ Leastways: 少なくとも、ともかく
❻ it's just a bit of ...: 単にちょっとした〜です
❼ offhandedly: ぶっきらぼうに
❽ leaned forward: 身を乗り出した

「わしもインドに行ってみたいね」と老人は言った。「ちょっと見て回るのもいい」
「いえ、ここが一番です」と特務曹長は首を横に振った。空のグラスを置いて、ふっとため息をつき、また首を横に振った。
「見てみたいね、古い寺院とか苦行僧とか大道芸人とか」と老人は言った。「それはそうとモリス、このあいだ言いかけた、猿の手がどうこうという話、あれは何だね？」
「何でもありません」と軍人はあわてて言った。「ともかく、話すほどのものじゃありません」
「猿の手？」とホワイト夫人が好奇心をそそられて言った。
「ま、いわゆる魔術というようなやつでして」と特務曹長はぶっきらぼうに言った。
　三人の聞き手は熱心に身を乗り出した。訪問者はぼんやりと空のグラスを

❾ absent-mindedly: ぼんやりと、うわの空で

down again. His host filled it for him.

'❶To look at,' said the sergeant-major, ❷fumbling in his pocket, 'it's just an ordinary little paw, ❸dried to a mummy.'

He took something out of his pocket and proffered it. Mrs. White drew back ❹with a grimace, but her son, taking it, examined it curiously.

'And what is there special about it?' inquired Mr. White as he took it from his son, and having examined it, placed it upon the table.

'It ❺had a spell put on it by an old fakir,' said the sergeant-major, 'a very holy man. He wanted to show that ❻fate ruled people's lives, and that ❼those who interfered with it did so to their sorrow. He put a spell on it so that three separate men ❽could each have three wishes from it.'

His manner was so ❾impressive that his hearers were conscious that their light laughter ❿jarred somewhat.

❶ To look at: 見た目には、見たところ
❷ fumbling <fumble: もぞもぞと探る
❸ dried to a mummy: 乾いてミイラ化して
❹ with a grimace: しかめ面で、顔を歪めて。
❺ had a spell put on it: 魔法をかけられていた。put a spell on ... という形でよく使う。
❻ fate ruled people's lives: 人間の生涯は運命が支配している
❼ those who interfered with it did so to their sorrow: それ（運命）に干渉する者は、そうすることで悲しみを味わうことになる
❽ could each have three wishes from it: それぞれ三つの願いを叶えてもらえる
❾ impressive: 堂々とした。「印象的」と訳されがちだがそぐわないことが多い。「印

唇に持っていき、また下ろした。あるじが酒を注いでやった。

「見た目には」と特務曹長はポケットを探りながら言った。「何の変哲もない、乾いてミイラになった手です」

そうしてポケットから何かを取り出し、皆に差し出した。ホワイト夫人は顔をしかめて身を引いたが、息子はそれを受け取り、興味深げに眺め回した。

「で、これの何が特別なのかね？」とホワイト氏は、それを息子から受け取って眺め回したのちテーブルに置いて訊ねた。

「老いた苦行僧が魔法をかけたのです」と特務曹長は言った。「大変に徳の高い方でした。人間の生涯は運命に支配されているのだ、運命に逆らおうとする者はひどい目に遭うのだということをその方は示そうとしたのです。そこで猿の手に魔力を施し、三人の人間が、それぞれ三つの願いを叶えてもらえるようにしたのです」

堂々として大真面目なその態度に、三人の聞き手は、自分たちがうっかり笑い声を上げたのをいささか気まずく思った。

象的」はむしろ striking あたりか。
⑩ jar(red): 食い違う、調和を欠く

'Well, ❶why don't you have three, sir?' said Herbert White, ❷cleverly.

The soldier regarded him ❸in the way that middle age is wont to regard presumptuous youth. 'I have,' he said, quietly, and ❹his blotchy face whitened.

'And did you really have the three wishes ❺granted?' asked Mrs. White.

'I did,' said the sergeant-major, and his glass ❻tapped against his strong teeth.

'And has anybody else wished?' ❼persisted the old lady.

'The first man had his three wishes. Yes,' was the reply; 'I don't know what the first two were, but the third was for death. That's how I got the paw.'

His tones were so grave that ❽a hush fell upon the group.

'If you've had your three wishes, ❾it's no good to you now, then, Morris,' said the old man at last. 'What do you keep it for?'

❶ Why don't you have three: あなたが三つ叶えてもらえばいいじゃないですか
❷ cleverly: 才気走って。clever(ly) は「小賢しい」といった否定的な含みがあることが多い。
❸ in the way that middle age is wont to regard presumptuous youth: 中年が生意気な（presumptuous）若者を見る（regard）ときの常である見方で。be wont to ...: ～するのを常とする
❹ his blotchy face whitened: しみのある顔が蒼白になった
❺ grant(ed): ～を叶える
❻ tapped against his strong teeth: 頑丈な歯に当たっ（てカチンと鳴っ）た
❼ persist(ed): なおも追及する
❽ a hush fell upon the group: 一同に沈黙が降りた
❾ it's no good to you now, then: それじゃあ（then）、もう（now）君には役

「じゃああなたも三つの願いをかけてみたらいかがです？」ハーバート・ホワイトがすかさず言った。

生意気な若者を中年の人間が見るときによく見せる目付きで、軍人はハーバートを見た。「もうやりました」と彼は静かに言い、しみの多い顔が蒼白になった。

「それで、本当に三つの願いが叶いましたの？」とホワイト夫人が訊ねた。

「はい」と特務曹長は言った。グラスが頑丈な歯にかちんとぶつかった。

「ほかにも願いをかけた人はいるのですか？」と老いた夫人はなおも訊いた。

「はい、一人目の男も三つ願いが叶いました」という答えだった。「はじめの二つが何だったかは知りませんが、三つ目の願いは死ぬことでした。それで私がこれを手に入れたのです」

そのあまりの重々しい口調に、一同は思わず黙りこくった。

「じゃあ三つの願いは叶えてもらったわけだから、君にはもう役に立たんのだろう」と老人がようやく口を開いた。「なぜまだ手放さずに持っているんだね？」

に立たないんだな

The soldier shook his head. '❶Fancy, I suppose,' he said, slowly. 'I did have some idea of selling it, but I don't think I will. It ❷has caused enough mischief already. Besides, people won't buy. They think it's a fairy tale; some of them, and those who do ❸think anything of it want to try it first and pay me afterward.'

'If you could have another three wishes,' said the old man, ❹eyeing him keenly, 'would you have them?'

'I don't know,' said the other. 'I don't know.'

He took the paw, and ❺dangling it between his forefinger and thumb, suddenly threw it upon the fire. White, with a slight cry, ❻stooped down and snatched it off.

'Better let it burn,' said the soldier, ❼solemnly.

'If you don't want it, Morris,' said the other, 'give it to me.'

'I won't,' said his friend, ❽doggedly. 'I threw it on the fire. If you keep it, don't blame me for what happens. ❾Pitch it on the fire again ❿like a sensible man.'

❶ Fancy: 気まぐれ
❷ has caused enough mischief already: もう十分害を及ぼした
❸ think anything of it: それ（猿の手）に少しでも価値を認める。*I don't think much of this book.*（この本は大したことないと思う）
❹ eyeing him keenly: 彼を食い入るように見て
❺ dangling <dangle: ～をぶら下げる
❻ stooped down and snatched it off: かがんでそれをひっ摑んだ
❼ solemnly: 厳粛に、重々しく
❽ doggedly: 執拗に、しぶとく
❾ Pitch: ～を投げる
❿ like a sensible man: 分別ある人間のように＝馬鹿な真似はせずに

軍人は首を横に振った。「ただの気まぐれでしょうね」と彼はゆっくり言った。「実際、売ろうかと考えたこともあるのですが、まあ売らないでしょうね。もうこいつは十分害悪をまき散らしましたから。それに、買う人なんていやしません。みんなおとぎばなしだと思うか、そうでなけりゃ、いちおう本気にしてもまず先に試したがって、金を払うのはそのあとだと言うんです」

「もう一度三つ願いをかけられるとしたら」と老人は男をじっと見据えながら言った。「かけたいと思うかね？」

「どうでしょうか」と相手は言った。「どうでしょうかねえ」

彼は猿の手を摑んで、親指と人差し指でつまんでぶら下げていたが、いきなりそれを暖炉の炎のなかに投げ込んだ。あっと小さく叫んで、ホワイト氏はあわててかがんで手を暖炉から引っぱり出した。

「燃やしてしまった方がいいですよ」と軍人は厳(いか)めしく言った。

「君が要らんのなら、私にくれたまえ」と老人は言った。

「いいえ」と相手はなおも言った。「私はそいつを火にくべたんです。あなたがお持ちになるんなら、何が起ころうと私を責めないでいただきたい。妙な気は起こさずに、暖炉に捨てておしまいなさい」

The other shook his head and examined his new possession ❶closely. 'How do you do it?' he inquired.

'Hold it up in your right hand and ❷wish aloud,' said the sergeant-major, 'but ❸I warn you of the consequences.'

'Sounds like the *Arabian Nights*,' said Mrs. White, as she rose and began to set the supper. 'Don't you think you might wish for four pairs of hands for me?'

Her husband drew ❹the talisman from pocket, and then all three ❺burst into laughter as the sergeant-major, with a look of alarm on his face, caught him by the arm.

'If you must wish,' he said, ❻gruffly, 'wish for something sensible.'

Mr. White dropped it back in his pocket, and placing chairs, motioned his friend to the table. ❼In the business of supper the talisman was partly forgotten, and afterward the three sat listening ❽in an enthralled fashion to ❾a second instalment of the soldier's

❶ closely: じっと、注意深く
❷ wish aloud: 願い事を声に出して言う
❸ I warn you of the consequences: そこから何が起きるか、警告しますからね。consequence(s) はつねに訳しづらい言葉だが、何かをした結果として起きる波紋、新たな事態のこと。
❹ the talisman: お守り、不思議な力のあるもの。ここでは猿の手のこと。
❺ burst into laughter: ゲラゲラ笑い出した
❻ gruffly: 荒っぽい声で
❼ In the business of supper: 夕食をとるなかで
❽ in an enthralled fashion: 夢中になって。fashion は way や manner に同じ。
❾ a second instalment: 二回目の分。instalment は連載や分割払いの一回分の意。

老人は首を横に振って、手に入れたばかりの品をじっくりと眺めた。「これ、どうやるのかね？」と彼は訊ねた。

「右手で持ってかざして、願いごとを口にするのです」と特務曹長は言った。「ですが、警告します、何が起きるかわかりませんよ」

「『アラビアン・ナイト』みたいねえ」とホワイト夫人が、夕食を並べにかかろうと席を立ちながら言った。「あなた、あたしに手を四人分与えたまえ、って祈ってくれたら？」

夫がまじないの道具をポケットから取り出すと、三人ともわっと笑い出したが、特務曹長は顔に恐怖の表情を浮かべて老人の腕を摑んだ。

「どうしても願いごとをするというのなら、まともな願いにしてください」と彼はつっけんどんに言った。

ホワイト氏はそれをポケットに戻し、椅子を動かしながら友人を食卓に手招きした。夕食が進行するとともにまじない具はなかば忘れられ、食後三人

adventures in India.

'❶If the tale about the monkey's paw is not more truthful than those he has been telling us,' said Herbert, as ❷the door closed behind their guest, just in time for him to catch the last train, '❸we shan't make much out of it.'

'Did you give him anything for it, father?' inquired Mrs. White, regarding her husband closely.

'❹A trifle,' said he, ❺colouring slightly. 'He didn't want it, but I made him take it. And he ❻pressed me again to throw it away.'

'❼Likely,' said Herbert, with pretended horror. 'Why, we're going to be rich, and famous and happy. Wish to be an emperor, father, ❽to begin with; then you can't be ❾henpecked.'

He darted round the table, pursued by the ❿maligned Mrs. White ⓫armed with an antimacassar.

Mr. White took the paw from his pocket and ⓬eyed it dubiously. 'I don't know what to wish for, and that's a fact,' he

❶ If the tale about the monkey's paw is not more truthful than those he has been telling us: 猿の手の話が、いま彼が話していたいろんな話よりも真実でないならば＝いまの話みたいに眉唾ものだったら
❷ the door closed behind their guest: 客が出ていったあとにドアが閉まった。He closed the door behind him が時おり「彼はうしろ手にドアを閉めた」と訳されたりするが、単に「ドアの外に出て、閉めた」あるいは「ドアから中に入って、閉めた」ということであって、「うしろ手」という特殊な閉め方があるわけではない。
❸ we sha'nt make much of it: そこから大したものは得られまい。shan't: shall not
❹ A trifle: わずかの金額
❺ colour(ing): 赤面する

は軍人のインド冒険談にふたたび聴き入った。
「猿の手の話も、いまのいろんな話同様に眉唾ものでしょうかねえ」とハーバートは、最終列車にぎりぎり間に合う時間に客が出ていって玄関のドアが閉まったところで言った。「だとしたら大して効き目もなさそうですね」
「あなた、お礼に何か差し上げたの？」とホワイト夫人は夫の顔をまじまじと見ながら言った。
「はした金さ」と夫はわずかに顔を赤らめて答えた。「要らないと言ったんだが、まあそう言わずに、と受け取らせたんだ。そしたらまた、捨ててしまいなさい、と言われたよ」
「そりゃそうでしょうよ」とハーバートは、ぞっとしたような顔を装って言った。「何せ僕らは、金持ちに、有名に、幸福になるんだから。父さん、まずは、我を皇帝にしたまえって祈りなさいよ。そうすりゃ母さんの尻の下にも敷かれなくなりますよ」
いわれなき非難を浴びたホワイト夫人が椅子カバーを手に追いかけ、ハーバートはテーブルを回り込んで逃げていった。
ホワイト氏はポケットから猿の手を取り出し、疑わしげな目で眺めた。「何を願ったらいいかわからんなあ、実際」と彼はゆっくり言った。「欲しいも

❻ press(ed): ～に強いる、強く促す
❼ Likely: ありそうなことだ＝そりゃそうでしょうよ
❽ to begin with: 手始めに
❾ henpeck(ed):（妻が夫を）尻に敷く
❿ malign(ed): ～を中傷する
⓫ armed with an antimacassar: 椅子カバーで武装して。antimacassar は椅子などの汚れ防止と飾りを兼ねた覆い。
⓬ eyed it dubiously: 疑わしげな目でそれを見た

said, slowly. 'It seems to me I've got all I want.'

'❶If you only cleared the house, you'd be quite happy, wouldn't you?' said Herbert, with his hand on his shoulder. 'Well, wish for two hundred pounds, then; ❷that'll just do it.'

His father, ❸smiling shamefacedly at his own credulity, held up the talisman, as his son, with a solemn face, ❹somewhat marred by a wink at his mother, sat down at the piano and struck a few impressive chords.

'I wish for ❺two hundred pounds,' said the old man distinctly.

❻A fine crash from the piano greeted the words, interrupted by ❼a shuddering cry from the old man. His wife and son ran toward him.

'It moved,' he cried, with ❽a glance of disgust at the object as it lay on the floor.

'As I wished, it twisted in my hand like a snake.'

'Well, I don't see the money,' said his son as he picked it up

❶ If you only cleared the house: 家の借金さえ済ませたら
❷ that'll just do it: それで足りるはずだ、間に合うはずだ
❸ smiling shamefacedly at his own credulity: 自分の信じやすさを恥じるように笑って
❹ somewhat marred by a wink at his mother: 母親に向けたウィンクによっていささか損なわれて。せっかく物々しい顔（a solemn face）をしたのに、ということ。
❺ two hundred pounds: Bank of Englandが提供しているinflation calculatorによれば、2020年の25,139ポンド13ペンスに相当する（3,797,265円）。
❻ A fine crash: ジャジャーンという派手な音
❼ a shuddering cry: ぶるっという身震いを伴った叫び声
❽ a glance of disgust: 嫌悪の目

のはもうみんな持ってる気がする」

「これであとは家の借金が片付いたら、何の不満もないでしょう？」とハーバートは、父の肩に片手を置きながら言った。「だったら、二百ポンドを与えたまえって願いなさいよ。それで片がつきます」

自分のお目出度さに我ながら恥じ入るように苦笑しながら、父親がまじないの品をかざすと、息子は厳(おごそ)かな表情を浮かべつつも母親に向けてこっそり目配せを送り、ピアノの前に座ってドラマチックな和音をいくつか叩き出した。

「我に二百ポンドを与えたまえ」と老人ははっきりと口にした。

ダダーン、と堂々たるピアノの響きが応えたが、ぶるっと震えた老人の上げた叫び声でそれも断ち切られた。妻と息子が彼のもとに駆け寄った。

「動いたんだ」と彼は、床に転がった手を嫌悪もあらわに一瞥(べつ)しながら叫んだ。「願いをかけたとたん、蛇みたいに手のなかでするっとよじれたんだ」

「二百ポンド、出てこないじゃないですか」と息子は言いながら、手を拾っ

and placed it on the table, 'and ❶I bet I never shall.'

'It must have been your ❷fancy, father,' said his wife, regarding him anxiously.

He shook his head. 'Never mind, though; ❸there's no harm done, but it gave me a shock ❹all the same.'

They sat down by the fire again while the two men finished their pipes. Outside, the wind was higher than ever, and the old man ❺started nervously at the sound of a door banging upstairs. ❻A silence unusual and depressing settled upon all three, which lasted until the old couple rose ❼to retire for the night.

'I expect you'll find the cash tied up in a big bag in the middle of your bed,' said Herbert, as he ❽bade them good-night, 'and something horrible ❾squatting up on top of the wardrobe watching you as you pocket ❿your ill-gotten gains.'

He sat alone in the darkness, gazing at the dying fire, and seeing faces in it. The last face was so horrible and so ⓫simian

❶ I bet: I'm sure
❷ fancy: 気のせい
❸ there's no harm done: 何も危害は為されていない、害はない
❹ all the same: それでも、やはり
❺ start(ed): ハッとする
❻ A silence ... settled upon all three: 沈黙が三人を包んだ
❼ to retire for the night: 今夜はもう寝ようと
❽ bade them good-night: お休みなさいと言った。bade は bid の過去形。
❾ squat(ting): しゃがむ
❿ your ill-gotten gains: あなたが邪(よこしま)な手段で得た富。おどけて物々しく言っている。
⓫ simian: 猿のような

てテーブルの上に置いた。「いつまで待っても出てきやしませんね」

「きっと気のせいよ、あなた」と妻は、心配げに夫を見ながら言った。

夫は首を横に振った。「まあどうでもいいさ。何かあったわけじゃないんだし。でもぎょっとさせられたがな」

三人はふたたび暖炉の前に座り、男二人はパイプを吸い終えた。表ではいつにも増して風が強く、二階でドアがばたんと閉まる音が響くと老人は落着かなげにぎくっとした。いつになく重苦しい沈黙が三人を包み、そろそろ寝るかと夫婦が立ち上がるまで続いた。

「きっとベッドの真ん中に大きな袋があって、紐を解いたら中に金が入ってますよ」とハーバートは二人にお休みを告げながら言った。「で、洋服ダンスの上に何かおぞましいものがうずくまっていて、父さんがその穢(けが)れた金をふところに入れるのを見物してるでしょうよ」

ハーバードは闇の中に一人座って、消えかけた火にじっと見入り、そこにいろんな顔を見ていた。最後の顔は何ともおぞましく、いかにも猿のようだっ

that he gazed at it in amazement. It got so vivid that, with a little uneasy laugh, he ❶felt on the table for a glass containing a little water to throw over it. His hand grasped the monkey's paw, and with a little shiver he wiped his hand on his ❷coat and went up to bed.

II.

In the brightness of the ❸wintry sun next morning as it ❹streamed over the breakfast table he laughed at his fears. There was ❺an air of prosaic wholesomeness about the room which it had lacked on the previous night, and the dirty, ❻shrivelled little paw was pitched on the sideboard with ❼a carelessness which ❽betokened no great belief in its ❾virtues.

'I suppose all old soldiers are the same,' said Mrs. White.

❶ felt on the table for a glass: コップを取ろうとテーブルの上を探った
❷ coat: この時代あたりまでは、coat が「コート」ではなく「上着」の意になることが多い。
❸ wintry: 冬の
❹ stream(ed): 流れ込む
❺ an air of prosaic wholesomeness: 平凡な健全さの雰囲気。おどろおどろしい考えなどを一笑に付す日常的な空気ということ。
❻ shrivelled: 萎びた
❼ a carelessness which betokened no great belief in its virtues: その効用をろくに信じていないことを伝えるぞんざいさ。
❽ betoken(ed): ～を物語る
❾ virtue(s): 効力、効き目

たので、ハーバードは愕然としてそれに見入った。顔があまりに生々しくなったものだから、不安げな笑い声を上げながら、水をかけようと、水が少し入ったグラスを取ろうとしてテーブルの上を手探りした。その手が猿の手を摑んでしまい、ハーバードは軽くぶるっと震えて、上着で手を拭き、寝室に上がっていった。

II.

翌朝、冬の眩しい太陽が朝の食卓に注ぎ込むなか、老人は自分の臆病さを笑った。昨日の晩にはなかった、ごく即物的な健全さがあたりに漂っていて、薄汚くしぼんだ小さな手は、その効験を誰も信じていないことを示すぞんざいさでもってサイドボードの上に放り投げられた。

「歳とった兵隊さんなんてみんな一緒ね」とホワイト夫人は言った。「あん

'❶The idea of our listening to such nonsense! How could wishes be granted in these days? And if they could, how could two hundred pounds hurt you, father?'

'Might drop on his head from the sky,' said the ❷frivolous Herbert.

'Morris said the things happened so naturally,' said his father, '❸that you might if you so wished attribute it to coincidence.'

'Well, don't ❹break into the money before I come back,' said Herbert as he rose from the table. 'I'm afraid it'll ❺turn you into a mean, avaricious man, and ❻we shall have to disown you.'

His mother laughed, and following him to the door, watched him down the road; and returning to the breakfast table, was very happy ❼at the expense of her husband's credulity. ❽All of which did not prevent her from ❾scurrying to the door at the postman's knock, nor prevent her from ❿referring somewhat shortly to ⓫retired sergeant-majors of bibulous habits when she found that

❶ The idea of our ...: 私たちが〜するなんて。憤慨・不満を伝える。"The idea!" だけでも「(そんなこと考えるなんて) とんでもない!」「ひどい!」という意になる。

❷ frivolous: 軽薄な

❸ that you might if you so wished attribute it to coincidence: そうしたければ偶然のせいにできるように。if you so wished が挿入的に入っている。attribute A to B で「A を B のせいにする、B が原因だと考える」。

❹ break into ...: 〜に手をつける

❺ turn you into a mean, avaricious man: あなたを意地の悪い、強欲な人間に変えてしまう

❻ we shall have to disown you: あなたを勘当するしかなくなる、縁を切るしかなくなる。普通は親が子を disown することに基づく冗談。

なたわごとにみんなで聴き入ったなんて！　いまどき、おまじないで願いごとなんて叶うわけないじゃありませんか。でもまああなた、かりに叶ったって、二百ポンドもらえるなら害はないわよね」

「空から父さんの頭を直撃したりして」とハーバートがおどけて言った。

「すごく自然に起きるんだってモリスは言ってたな」と父親は言った。「偶然のせいだと思いたければ思えるくらいに」

「ま、僕が帰ってくるまで金には手をつけないでくださいよ」とハーバートは食卓から立ち上がりながら言った。「父さん、さもしい強欲男になっちゃ困りますよ、そしたら勘当ですからね」

母親があはははと笑い、玄関まで息子を送り出して、道路を歩いていくのを見送ってから朝の食卓に戻った。夫のお人好しぶりを息子と二人でからかって、夫人としてもおかしくて仕方なかった。それでも、郵便配達夫のノックが聞こえると夫人はいそいそと玄関に飛んでいった。が、来た手紙が仕立屋の請求書だとわかると、酒飲みの退役曹長がどうこう、といささか意地悪な文句を口にした。

❼ at the expense of ...: 〜をダシにして

❽ All of which did not prevent her from ...: こうしたすべても、彼女が〜するのを妨げはしなかった。夫のお目出度さを笑っておきながら、いざ郵便配達が来ると……ということ。

❾ scurry(ing): いそいそ、せかせかと走る

❿ referring somewhat shortly to ...: いささかぶっきらぼうに〜のことを言って。shortly: 無愛想に

⓫ retired sergeant-majors of bibulous habits: 酒好きの退役した特務曹長

❶the post brought a tailor's bill.

'Herbert ❷will have some more of his funny remarks, I expect, when he comes home,' she said, as they ❸sat at dinner.

'❹I dare say,' said Mr. White, ❺pouring himself out some beer; 'but ❻for all that, the thing moved in my hand; ❼that I'll swear to.'

'You thought it did,' said the old lady ❽soothingly.

'I say it did,' replied the other. 'There was no thought about it; I had just—What's the matter?'

His wife made no reply. She was watching the mysterious movements of a man outside, who, ❾peering in an undecided fashion at the house, appeared to be trying to make up his mind to enter. ❿In mental connection with the two hundred pounds, she noticed that the stranger was well dressed, and wore a silk hat ⓫of glossy newness. Three times he paused at the gate, and then ⓬walked on again. The fourth time he stood with his hand upon it, and then ⓭with sudden resolution ⓮flung it open and walked

❶ the post: 郵便物
❷ will have some more of his funny remarks: きっとまた（いつもの彼のように）おどけたことを言うだろう
❸ sat at dinner: dinner は一日の一番主たる食事という意味であり、夕食とは限らない。この時代あたりまでは昼食のことが多い。
❹ I dare say: まあそうだろうね
❺ pouring himself out some beer: 自分にビールを注いで。out はなくてもあまり変わらない。
❻ for all that: そうは言っても、とはいえ
❼ that I'll swear to: I'll swear to that という普通の語順より強い響き。
❽ soothingly: なだめるように
❾ peering in an undecided fashion: 決めかねている様子で覗いて

「帰ってきたらまたハーバートにからかわれるわよ」と彼女は昼食の席につきながら言った。
「だろうな」とホワイト氏は自分のグラスにビールを注ぎながら言った。「それでもやっぱり、あれは本当に、この手のなかで動いたんだ。神にかけて誓う」
「そう思っただけよ」老いた夫人はなだめるように言った。
「動いたのさ」と夫は答えた。「思う思わないっていう話じゃない。私がちょうど——どうした？」
　妻は何とも答えなかった。表にいる男の奇妙な動きに彼女は見入っていた。どうしたらいいか決めかねたような様子で男は家のなかを覗いていて、入ってくる度胸を奮い起こそうとしているように見えた。夫人は二百ポンドに何となく連想が働き、見知らぬ人物が上等の服を着ていて真新しいシルクハットをかぶっていることに目をとめた。木戸のところで男は三度立ちどまり、そのたびにまた通り過ぎた。四度目に、やっと木戸に手をかけ、一気に肚(はら)を決めてさっと押し開け、玄関までの通路を歩いてきた。それと同時にホワイ

⑩ In mental connection with the two hundred pounds: 200ポンドと頭のなかでつなげて
⑪ of glossy newness: ぴかぴかに新しい
⑫ walked on: 先へ歩いていった
⑬ with sudden resolution: 突然意を決して
⑭ flung it open:（門を）パッと開けた

up ❶the path. Mrs. White at the same moment placed her hands behind her, and hurriedly ❷unfastening the strings of her apron, put ❸that useful article of apparel beneath the cushion of her chair.

She brought the stranger, who ❹seemed ill at ease, into the room. He gazed at her ❺furtively, and listened ❻in a preoccupied fashion as the old lady apologised for the appearance of the room, and her husband's coat, ❼a garment which he usually reserved for the garden. She then waited ❽as patiently as her sex would permit, for him to ❾broach his business, but he was at first strangely silent.

'I—was asked to call,' he said at last, and stooped and picked a piece of cotton from his trousers. 'I come from "Maw and Meggins."'

The old lady started. 'Is anything the matter?' she asked, breathlessly. 'Has anything happened to Herbert? What is it? What is it?'

Her husband ❿interposed. '⓫There, there, mother,' he said,

❶ the path: 門から家までの通路のこと。
❷ unfasten(ing): ～を外す、ほどく
❸ that useful article of apparel: 直訳は「その有用な衣料品」。「エプロン」のやや持って回った言い換え。
❹ seemed ill at ease: 落ち着かないようだった
❺ furtively: こっそり
❻ in a preoccupied fashion: うわの空の様子で
❼ a garment which he usually reserved for the garden: ふだんは庭仕事に使っている衣服。夫の上着のくたびれた様子を言い訳している。
❽ as patiently as her sex would permit: 直訳は「女性であることが許す限り辛抱強く」。女性であることは人に辛抱強さを許さない＝女性は辛抱強くない、という前提に立った物言い。

ト夫人は両手をうしろに回し、エプロンの紐を急いで外して、椅子のクッションの下にその有用なる衣料を押し込んだ。

おどおど落着かぬ様子の見知らぬ男を夫人は部屋に案内した。男はこっそりとホワイト夫人の顔色を窺(うかが)い、散らかっていて済みませんねえ、主人もこんな庭仕事の格好で失礼します、と夫人が詫びるのを上の空で聞いている。それから夫人は、相手が話を切り出すのを、女としてのたしなみを精一杯示して辛抱強く待ったが、相手ははじめ、何とも不可解に押し黙っていた。

「私——使いの者でございまして」と彼はやっと言い、身をかがめてズボンについた糸屑をつまみ上げた。「モー・アンド・メギンズ社から参りました」

老いた夫人はぎくっと身構えた。「何かあったんでしょうか？」と彼女は息を殺して訊ねた。「ハーバートに何かあったんですか？　何なんです？何なんです？」

夫が割って入った。「まあまあ、お前」とせわしなく言った。「お座りなさ

❾ broach his business: 用件を切り出す
❿ interpose(d): 口をはさむ
⓫ There, there: まあまあ。人をなだめる言い方。

hastily. 'Sit down, and don't ❶jump to conclusions. You've not brought bad news, I'm sure, sir;' and he eyed the other ❷wistfully.

'I'm sorry—' began the visitor.

'Is he hurt?' ❸demanded the mother, wildly.

The visitor ❹bowed in assent. 'Badly hurt,' he said, quietly, 'but he is not in any pain.'

'Oh, thank God!' said the old woman, ❺clasping her hands. 'Thank God for that! Thank—'

She ❻broke off suddenly as ❼the sinister meaning of the assurance ❽dawned upon her and she ❾saw the awful confirmation of her fears in the other's averted face. She caught her breath, and ❿turning to her slower-witted husband, laid her trembling old hand upon his. There was a long silence.

'He was caught in the machinery,' said the visitor ⓫at length in a low voice.

'Caught in the machinery,' repeated Mr. White, in a ⓬dazed

❶ jump to conclusions: 早まった結論を下す、早合点する
❷ wistfully: 切なそうに、すがるように
❸ demand(ed): 問いただす、答えを迫る
❹ bowed in assent: そうですと言うように一礼した。assent: 同意
❺ clasping her hands: 両手をぎゅっと握って
❻ broke off: 急に黙った
❼ the sinister meaning of the assurance: "but he is not in any pain" という、パッと聞くと assurance（保証、請けあい）に思える言葉から読みとれる不吉な意味、ということ。
❽ dawned upon her:（真相などが）見えてきた、わかった
❾ saw the awful confirmation of her fears in the other's averted face: 直訳は「相手のそらした顔の中に、自分の恐怖の恐ろしい裏付けを見た」。

い、早合点しちゃいけないよ。ねえあなた、べつに悪い知らせじゃありませんよね」と、客の方にすがるような目を向けた。

「申し訳ございません——」と訪問者は切り出した。

「怪我したんですか？」と母親が問いつめる。

そうですと答える代わりに訪問者は頭を下げた。「ひどい怪我をされました」と静かに言った。「ですがもう、痛みを覚えてはいらっしゃいません」

「まあ、よかった」と老いた女性は言って、両手を握り締めた。「ほんとによかった！　ほんとに——」

もう痛みはない、という言葉の禍々(まがまが)しい意味に思い当たって、彼女は不意に口をつぐんだ。相手が顔をそらしているその姿に、自分の恐れのおぞましい裏付けを彼女は見てとった。息を呑んで、まだ気づかずにいる夫の方に向き直り、震える老いた手を彼の手に載せた。長い沈黙があった。

「機械に体をはさまれたのです」と訪問者はやっとのことで、低い声で言った。

「機械に体をはさまれた」とホワイト氏は鸚鵡(おうむ)返しに言った。「そうですか」

⑩ turning to her slower-witted husband: 自分より呑み込みの悪い夫の方を向いて
⑪ at length: at last
⑫ dazed: 茫然とした

fashion, 'yes.'

He sat ❶staring blankly out at the window, and taking his wife's hand between his own, pressed it ❷as he had been wont to do ❸in their old courting-days nearly forty years before.

'He was the only one left to us,' he said, turning gently to the visitor. 'It is hard.'

The other coughed, and rising, walked slowly to the window. '❹The firm wished me to ❺convey their sincere sympathy with you in your great loss,' he said, without looking round. 'I beg that you will understand I am only their servant and merely obeying orders.'

There was no reply; the old woman's face was white, her eyes staring, and her breath ❻inaudible; on the husband's face was ❼a look such as his friend the sergeant might have carried into his first action.

'❽I was to say that Maw and Meggins ❾disclaim all respon-

❶ staring blankly out at the window: 窓の方を茫然と見て。stare という言葉は仰天して何かに見入るときにも、空っぽの頭で特に何を見るともなく漠然と見るときにも使う（ここはどちらかといえば後者）。とにかく目がいつもより開いている感じ。13 行目の staring も同様。

❷ as he had been wont to do: as he used to do。wont は p. 22, l. 3 に同じ。

❸ in their old courting-days: 昔、まだ恋愛中だったころ

❹ The firm: 会社

❺ convey their sincere sympathy with you in your great loss: 直訳は「大きな喪失を被ったあなた方に対する心からの同情を伝える」。改まった紋切り型のお悔やみの言葉を言っていると思えば十分。

❻ inaudible: 聞き取れない

❼ a look such as his friend the sergeant might have carried into his first

氏は座ったまま虚ろな目で窓の方を見やり、それから、妻の手を自分の両手でくるんで、四十年近く前、まだ求婚中だったころよくそうしたようにぎゅっと握りしめた。

「私どもにはあの子しか残っていなかったのです」と氏は言って、穏やかに訪問者の方を向いた。「つらいことです」

相手は咳払いし、立ち上がってゆっくり窓際まで歩いていった。「ご子息を亡くされたこと、心からお悔やみ申し上げるよう社から託(ことづか)って参りました」と男は向き直らずに言った。「どうかご理解ください、私は一介の従業員でありまして、命令に従っているだけなのです」

返事はなかった。老いた女性は顔面蒼白で目は見開かれ、息も立てていなかった。夫の顔には、友人の曹長も生まれて初めての戦闘にこんな顔でつっ込んでいっただろうかと思える表情が浮かんでいた。

「モー・アンド・メギンズ社はいっさいの責任を否認する、とお伝えするよ

action: 直訳は「彼の友人の曹長が初めての戦闘に携えていったかもしれないような表情」。

❽ I was to say that ...: 私は～と言うように命じられました。be to ... はいろんな意味になりうるが、ここは命令・義務を表わす。

❾ disclaim:（責任などを）否定する。広告などに添えられた「但し書き」（これは～を保証するものではありません 等々）を disclaimer という。

sibility,' continued the other. 'They admit no ❶liability at all, but in consideration of your son's ❷services, they wish to present you with a certain sum as ❸compensation.'

Mr. White dropped his wife's hand, and rising to his feet, gazed with a look of horror at his visitor. His dry lips shaped the words, 'How much?'

'Two hundred pounds,' was the answer.

❹Unconscious of his wife's shriek, the old man smiled faintly, put out his hands like a ❺sightless man, and dropped, ❻a senseless heap, to the floor.

III.

In the huge new ❼cemetery, ❽some two miles distant, the old people ❾buried their dead, and came back to a house ❿steeped in

❶ liability: 責任、義務
❷ service(s): 功労、功績
❸ compensation: 補償、埋めあわせ
❹ Unconscious of his wife's shriek: 妻の悲鳴も意識に入らず
❺ sightless: 目の見えない
❻ a senseless heap: 意識のないかたまりとなって
❼ (a) cemetery: 墓地
❽ some two miles distant: 2 マイルほど離れている。some は about の意。
❾ buried their dead: 死者を埋葬した。行為に見合った、厳かな紋切り型。
❿ steeped in shadow and silence: 影と沈黙に包まれて

う仰せつかって参りました」と相手は先を続けた。「社としては何ら賠償義務は認めておりませんが、ご子息のこれまでのご貢献に鑑みて、一定の金額を補償金としてお支払いしたいと考えております」

ホワイト氏は妻の手を放し、立ち上がって、恐怖の目で訪問者を見つめた。乾いた唇が言葉を形作った。「いくらです？」

「二百ポンドです」と答えが返ってきた。

妻の悲鳴も耳に入らず、老人はかすかな笑みを浮かべ、盲人のように両手を前につき出し、意識を失って床に倒れ込んだ。

Ⅲ.

二マイルばかり離れた新しい巨大な墓地で老夫婦は死者を埋葬し、影と沈黙に包まれた家に帰ってきた。何もかもがあわただしく過ぎていき、はじめ

shadow and silence. ❶It was all over so quickly that at first they could hardly realise it, and ❷remained in a state of expectation as though of something else to happen— ❸something else which was to lighten this load, too heavy for old hearts to bear.

But the days passed, and expectation ❹gave place to resignation— ❺the hopeless resignation of the old, ❻sometimes miscalled apathy. Sometimes they hardly exchanged a word, for now they had nothing to talk about, and ❼their days were long to weariness.

It was about a week after that the old man, waking suddenly in the night, stretched out his hand and found himself alone. The room was in darkness, and ❽the sound of subdued weeping came from the window. He raised himself in bed and listened.

'Come back,' he said, tenderly. 'You will be cold.'

'It is colder for my son,' said the old woman, and ❾wept afresh.

❿The sound of her sobs died away on his ears. The bed was

❶ It was all over so quickly: すべてがあっという間に済んだ。"It's/It was all over" で定型句。
❷ remained in a state of expectation:（終わったという実感が持てず）何かを待ち受ける状態に留まっていた
❸ something else which was to lighten this load: この重荷を軽くしてくれる何かほかのもの。この be to ... は「〜するはずの」といった意味合い。
❹ gave place to resignation: 諦めに場所を譲った＝諦めに変わった
❺ the hopeless resignation of the old: 年とった人間特有の希望なき諦め。the old は the old people の意（the+ 形容詞で「〜な人々」の意味になる）。
❻ sometimes miscalled apathy: 時に「無関心」と間違って呼ばれている
❼ their days were long to weariness: 日々は weariness（疲労・倦怠）に至るほど長かった

はろくに実感もなく、二人とも、何かまだほかのことが——この重荷を、老いた心が耐えるにはあまりに重い荷を軽くしてくれる何かが——起きるのを期待しているような心持ちだった。

だが日々は過ぎていき、期待は諦念に、時に無関心と誤って呼ばれたりもする老人特有の望みなき諦念に変わっていった。ほとんど何も言葉を交わさないときもあった。話すことなど何もないのだ。日々はうんざりするほど長かった。

それから一週間ほど過ぎて、老人が夜中にふと目覚めて手を伸ばすと、寝床には自分しかいなかった。寝室は真っ暗で、押し殺したすすり泣きの声が窓辺から聞こえてきた。彼はベッドで身を起こし、泣き声に聴き入った。

「戻っておいで、そんな寒いところにいたら風邪をひくよ」と彼は優しく言った。

「あの子はもっと寒いところにいるのよ」と老いた妻は言って、またしくしく泣き出した。

すすり泣く声が、夫の耳から遠のいていった。寝床は暖かかったし、眠気

❽ the sound of subdued weeping: 抑えられた泣き声
❾ wept afresh: また新たに涙した
❿ The sound of her sobs died away on his ears: 直訳は「妻のすすり泣きは夫の耳で死んでいった」。died away on ... は p. 14, ll. 11-12 に同じ。

warm, and his eyes heavy with sleep. He ❶dozed fitfully, and then slept until a sudden wild cry from his wife ❷awoke him with a start.

'*The paw!*' she cried wildly. 'The monkey's paw!'

He ❸started up in alarm. 'Where? Where is it? What's the matter?'

She came ❹stumbling across the room toward him. 'I want it,' she said, quietly. 'You've not destroyed it?'

'It's in the parlour, on ❺the bracket,' he replied, ❻marvelling. 'Why?'

She cried and laughed together, and bending over, kissed his cheek.

'❼I only just thought of it,' she said, hysterically. 'Why didn't I think of it before? Why didn't *you* think of it?'

'Think of what?' he questioned.

'The other two wishes,' she replied, rapidly. 'We've only had

❶ dozed fitfully: 切れぎれに浅く眠った
❷ awoke him with a start: はっと目を覚まさせた
❸ started up in alarm: ぎょっとして身を起こした。alarm は驚き・恐怖・狼狽が交じった感情。
❹ stumbling <stumble: よろよろ歩く
❺ the bracket: 張り出した棚、ランプを載せる台などを言う。
❻ marvel(ling): 驚く、いぶかる
❼ I only just thought of it: 今やっと思いついたのよ(もっと早く気付くべきだった、という含み)

で瞼が重かった。彼はうつらうつらとまどろみ、やがてすっかり寝入ったが、妻がいきなり狂おしく叫ぶ声でハッと目を覚ました。

「手よ！」と妻は狂おしく叫んでいた。「猿の手よ！」

夫はぎょっとして身を起こした。「どこだ？　どこにあるんだ？　どうした？」

妻はよろよろと夫の方に歩いてきた。「あれを頂戴」と静かな声で言った。「捨ててないわよね？」

「居間の、ランプ受けに置いてある」と夫は戸惑いつつ答えた。「なぜだね？」

妻は泣き声と笑い声を同時に上げ、かがみ込んで夫の頬にキスした。

「たったいま思いついたのよ」と彼女はほとんどヒステリー状態で言った。「どうしてもっと早く思いつかなかったのかしら？　どうしてあなた思いつかなかったの？」

「思いつくって、何を？」と夫は訊ねた。

「あと二つの願いごとよ」と妻は口早に答えた。「まだひとつしか叶えても

one.'

'Was not that enough?' ❶he demanded, fiercely.

'No,' she cried, ❷triumphantly; 'we'll have one more. Go down and get it quickly, and wish our boy alive again.'

The man sat up in bed and ❸flung the bedclothes from his quaking limbs. 'Good God, you are mad!' he cried, ❹aghast.

'Get it,' she ❺panted; 'get it quickly, and wish—Oh, my boy, my boy!'

Her husband struck a match and lit the candle. 'Get back to bed,' he said, ❻unsteadily. '❼You don't know what you are saying.'

'We had the first wish granted,' said the old woman, ❽feverishly; 'why not the second?'

'❾A coincidence,' ❿stammered the old man.

'Go and get it and wish,' cried his wife, ⓫quivering with excitement.

The old man turned and regarded her, and his voice shook. 'He

❶ he demanded, fiercely: 直訳は「荒々しく問いつめた」。ほとんど憤っているような様子。
❷ triumphantly: 勝ち誇って、意気揚々と
❸ flung the bedclothes from his quaking limbs: 震える手足から寝具を放り投げた
❹ aghast: ぞっとして
❺ pant(ed): あえぐように言う、息を切らして言う
❻ unsteadily: 不安定に、頼りなく
❼ You don't know what you are saying: 君は自分が何を言っているのかわかっていない=何を馬鹿なこと言っているんだ
❽ feverishly: 熱狂して、興奮して
❾ A coincidence: 偶然

らっていないのよ」

「あれでまだ足りんというのか？」と夫はかっとなって言い返した。

「そうよ」と妻は勝ち誇ったように叫んだ。「あとひとつ叶えてもらうのよ。早く取ってきてちょうだい、息子を生き返らせたまえって願うのよ」

夫は寝床で身を起こし、震える手足から寝具を払いのけた。「お前、気でも狂ったのか！」と愕然として叫んだ。

「持ってきて」と妻は息を切らしながら言った。「早く持ってきて、願いをかけるのよ——ああ、坊や、坊や！」

夫はマッチを擦って蠟燭に火を点けた。「寝床に戻りなさい」と上ずった声で言った。「馬鹿を言うんじゃない」

「最初の願いは叶ったのよ」と老いた妻は熱狂して言った。「二つ目だって叶うはずよ」

「あれは偶然だったのさ」と老いた夫は口ごもり気味に言った。

「持ってきて、願いをかけてよ」と妻は興奮に声を震わせて言った。

老人は向き直ってじっと妻を見た。声が震えた。「あの子は死んで十日に

❿ stammer(ed): 口ごもりながら言う
⓫ quiver(ing): 震える

has been dead ten days, and besides he— ❶I would not tell you else, but—I could only recognise him by his clothing. ❷If he was too terrible for you to see then, how now?'

'Bring him back,' cried the old woman, and dragged him toward the door. 'Do you think I fear the child I have ❸nursed?'

He went down in the darkness, and ❹felt his way to the parlour, and then to ❺the mantelpiece. The talisman was in its place, and a horrible fear that the unspoken wish might bring his ❻mutilated son before him ❼ere he could escape from the room ❽seized upon him, and he caught his breath as he found that he had lost the direction of the door. His brow cold with sweat, he felt his way round the table, and ❾groped along the wall until he found himself in the small ❿passage with the ⓫unwholesome thing in his hand.

Even his wife's face seemed changed as he entered the room. It was white and ⓬expectant, and to his fears seemed to have an

❶ I would not tell you else, but ...: ほかの状況だったら言わないだろうが＝仕方ないから言うが
❷ If he was ... then, how now?: あのとき彼が～なんだったら、今はどうなのか？
❸ nurse(d): ～に乳を与える
❹ felt his way to the parlour: 手探りで居間まで行った
❺ the mantelpiece: 炉棚
❻ mutilated: 無残に損なわれた
❼ ere: before の古い言い方。ここではすぐ前に before が出てくるので、反復を避けてこの語を使っている。
❽ seized upon him: a horrible fear that ... seized upon him（～という恐怖が彼を捉えた）というつながり。

なる。それにあの子は——本当なら黙っているところなんだが——服を見てやっとあの子だとわかる姿だったんだよ。あのときすでに、お前には恐ろしくて見られたものではなかったんだ、だったらいまはどうなってる？」

「あの子を連れ戻して」老いた女性は叫んで、夫をドアの方に引っぱっていった。「自分の乳をあげて育てた子を怖がるとでも思うの？」

夫は闇のなかを階下に降りていき、手さぐりで居間まで行って、炉棚へ進んでいった。まじないの道具は置いたままのところにあった。と、いまだ口にしていない願いごとが聞き届けられて無残に切り刻まれた息子が彼が逃げ出す間もなく目の前に現われるのではないか、そんな激しい恐怖に襲われて、ドアがどっちの方向にあるかもわからなくなっていることに気づいて思わず息が止まった。冷たい汗を額に浮かべて、手探りで食卓を回っていき、壁伝いに進んで、手におぞましい代物を持ったまま狭い戸口に出た。

寝室に入っていくと、妻の顔まで変わったように見えた。蒼白の、期待に満ちたその顔には、何か自然でない表情が浮かんでいるように思えて夫はぞっとした。妻のことが怖かった。

❾ groped along the wall: 壁に手探りしながら進んだ。felt が groped に変わっていっそう「手探り感」が増す。
❿ (a) passage: 通路、通り道
⓫ unwholesome: 不健全な、有害な
⓬ expectant: 期待している、待ち受けている

❶unnatural look upon it. He was afraid of her.

'*Wish!*' she cried, in a strong voice.

'It is foolish and ❷wicked,' he ❸faltered.

'*Wish!*' repeated his wife.

He raised his hand. 'I wish my son alive again.'

The talisman fell to the floor, and he regarded it fearfully. Then he ❹ sank trembling into a chair as the old woman, with burning eyes, walked to the window and raised the blind.

He sat until he was chilled with the cold, ❺glancing occasionally at the figure of the old woman peering through the window. ❻The candle-end, which had burned below ❼the rim of the china candlestick, was throwing ❽pulsating shadows on the ceiling and walls, until, with ❾a flicker larger than the rest, it ❿expired. The old man, with an unspeakable sense of relief at the failure of the talisman, ⓫crept back to his bed, and a minute or two afterward the old woman came silently and ⓬apathetically beside him.

❶ unnatural:「不自然な」というよりもっとずっと意味が強く、最低「異様な」くらい。

❷ wicked: 邪な、邪悪な（/wíkəd/ と読む）

❸ falter(ed):（声が）震える、口ごもる

❹ sank trembling into a chair: 震えながら椅子にどさっと沈み込んだ

❺ glancing ... at the figure of the old woman: 夫がもはや妻のことを妻と見ていないような書き方。

❻ The candle-end: 蠟燭の端

❼ the rim of the china candlestick: 磁器の蠟燭差しの縁

❽ pulsating shadows: 脈打つ影

❾ a flicker:（明かりの）ゆらめき

❿ expire(d): 消える

「願いをかけて！」と妻は力強い声で叫んだ。

「愚かな、邪(よこしま)なことだよ」と夫はおろおろ言った。

「願いをかけて！」と妻はくり返した。

夫は右手を上げた。「息子を生き返らせたまえ」

まじないの道具は床に落ち、夫はぶるっと身震いしてそれを眺めた。彼が震えながら椅子に沈み込むのをよそに、老いた妻は目をらんらんと輝かせて窓の方に行き、ブラインドを上げた。

窓の外をじっと覗き込むようにしている妻の方に時おり目をやりながら、夫は寒気(さむけ)に体が冷えてくるまで座っていた。いまや蠟燭も磁器製の蠟燭立てのへりより下まで短くなって、天井や壁にぴくぴくと脈打つ影を投げていたが、やがて、いつになく大きな炎をさっと上げて、消えてしまった。まじないが効かなかったことに心底ほっとして、老人は寝床に這い戻った。程なく妻も黙って戻ってきて、のろのろと隣に入ってきた。

⓫ crept <creep: 這う
⓬ apathetically: 何の感情も見せずに

Neither spoke, but lay silently listening to the ticking of the clock. A stair creaked, and ❶a squeaky mouse scurried noisily through the wall. The darkness was oppressive, and after lying for some time ❷screwing up his courage, he took the box of matches, and striking one, went downstairs for a candle.

At the foot of the stairs the match ❸went out, and he paused to strike another; and at the same moment a knock, ❹so quiet and stealthy as to be scarcely audible, sounded on the front door.

The matches fell from his hand and ❺spilled in the passage. He stood motionless, his breath suspended until the knock was repeated. Then he turned and ❻fled swiftly back to his room, and closed the door behind him. A third knock sounded through the house.

'*What's that?*' cried the old woman, ❼starting up.

'A rat,' said the old man in shaking tones—'a rat. ❽It passed me on the stairs.'

❶ a squeaky mouse scurried noisily: キーキーいう鼠が騒々しく走っていった
❷ screwing up his courage: 勇気を奮い起こして
❸ went out: 消えた
❹ so quiet and stealthy as to be scarcely audible: ひどく静かでひそやかで、ほとんど聞こえないくらい
❺ spill(ed): こぼれる
❻ fled <flee: 逃げる
❼ starting up: ハッと身を起こして。p. 50, l. 5 に同じ。
❽ It passed me on the stairs: 階段で私とすれ違った

二人とも何も言わずに黙って横たわり、時計がカチカチ鳴る音に耳を澄ましていた。階段がきしみ、壁のなかを鼠がキイッと騒々しく駆けていった。闇が重苦しく垂れた。しばらくのあいだ勇気を奮い起こそうとした末に、夫はマッチの箱を手に取り、一本擦って、階下に蠟燭を取りにいった。

階段を降りきったところでマッチが消えたので立ちどまってもう一本点けたのと同時に、ほとんど聞こえないほどの、ひどくひっそりしたノックの音が玄関で鳴った。

マッチが夫の手から落ち、ばらばらと通路に散らばった。彼はその場に、息も止まったまま凍りついていた。やがてノックがくり返された。彼は回れ右して寝室に舞い戻り、中に入るやドアを閉めた。三度目のノックが家中に響きわたった。

「あれは何？」と老いた妻がハッと身を起こして叫んだ。

His wife sat up in bed listening. A loud knock ❶resounded through the house.

'It's Herbert!' she screamed. 'It's Herbert!'

She ran to the door, but her husband was before her, and catching her by the arm, held her tightly.

'What are you going to do?' he whispered ❷hoarsely.

'It's my boy; it's Herbert!' she cried, ❸struggling mechanically. 'I forgot it was two miles away. What are you holding me for? ❹Let go. I must open the door.'

'❺For God's sake ❻don't let it in,' cried the old man, trembling.

'You're afraid of your own son,' she cried, struggling. 'Let me go. I'm coming, Herbert; I'm coming.'

There was another knock, and another. The old woman ❼with a sudden wrench broke free and ran from the room. Her husband followed to ❽the landing, and ❾called after her appealingly as she hurried downstairs. He ❿heard the chain rattle back and the

❶ resound(ed): 響きわたる
❷ hoarsely: しゃがれ声で、うわずった声で
❸ struggling mechanically: 直訳は「機械的に奮闘して」。もはや考える力がなくなった（あるいは、それを超えた）ふるまいという印象を与える。
❹ Let go: 離してちょうだい
❺ For God's sake: 頼むから。馬鹿な真似はよせ、という響き。
❻ don't let it in: やって来たものは妻には Herbert だが、夫には it である。
❼ with a sudden wrench broke free: 突然ぎゅっと体をねじって（夫の腕から）逃れた
❽ the landing: 踊り場。ここでは階段をのぼりきったところ。
❾ called after her: 妻の背中に呼びかけている感じ。
❿ heard the chain rattle back and the bottom bolt drawn: 鎖ががちゃが

「鼠だよ」と老人は震える声で言った。「鼠さ。階段ですれ違ったよ」

妻は寝床で頭を上げ、耳を澄ました。大きなノックの音が家中に轟いた。

「ハーバートよ！」と妻は金切り声を上げた。「ハーバートよ！」

彼女はドアめざして飛んでいこうとしたが、夫が彼女の前に立ちはだかり、その腕をしかと押さえつけた。

「どうしようというんだ？」と夫はしゃがれ声で囁いた。

「あたしの坊やよ、ハーバートよ！」と妻は、何も考えずに夫に抗いながら叫んだ。「二マイル離れてることを忘れていたわ。なぜ押さえるの？　放してちょうだい。ドアを開けてやらないと」

「よすんだ、入れちゃ駄目だ」と夫は身震いして叫んだ。

「自分の息子を怖がるなんて」と妻は抗いながら叫んだ。「放してよ。いま行くわよ、ハーバート。いま行くわ」

もう一度ノックの音がした。そしてもう一度。と、妻はぎゅっと身をよじらせて夫の手を振りほどき、部屋から飛び出していった。夫は階段の手前まで追いかけ、駆け下りていく彼女に必死に呼びかけた。チェーンががたがた

ちゃと外され、下の閂(かんぬき)が抜かれるのを聞いた

bottom bolt drawn slowly and stiffly from the socket. Then the old woman's voice, strained and panting.

'The bolt,' she cried, loudly. 'Come down. I can't reach it.'

But her husband was on his hands and knees groping wildly on the floor in search of the paw. ❶If he could only find it before the thing outside got in. ❷A perfect fusillade of knocks ❸reverberated through the house, and he heard the scraping of a chair as his wife put it down in the passage against the door. He heard the creaking of the bolt as it came slowly back, and at the same moment he found the monkey's paw, and ❹frantically breathed his third and last wish.

The knocking ceased suddenly, although the echoes of it were still in the house. He heard the chair drawn back, and the door opened. A cold wind rushed up the staircase, and ❺a long loud wail of disappointment and misery from his wife gave him courage to run down to her side, and then to the gate beyond. The street lamp flickering opposite shone on a quiet and deserted road.

❶ If he could only ...: 〜できさえしたら、何とか〜しないと
❷ A perfect fusillade of knocks: 直訳は「ノックの完璧な一斉射撃」。ガンガンガンガンガンという続けざまのノックが読んでいても聞こえてくる。
❸ reverberate(d): 反響する、響きわたる
❹ frantically breathed: 狂おしく口にした。breatheはささやくように言う感じ。
❺ a long loud wail: 長い、大きな嘆きの叫び

と外され、下の閂がゆっくり、ぎくしゃくと受け口から抜かれるのが聞こえた。やがて妻のふり絞った喘ぎ声が聞こえた。

「上の閂が！」と彼女は大声で叫んだ。「あなた、降りてきて！　あたしには届かないわ」

だが夫は手足をついて懸命に床を探り、猿の手を探していた。外にいるあれが中に入る前に何とか見つけないと。一斉射撃のごときノックの連打が家中に反響し、妻が椅子を引きずってきて玄関前に置くのが聞こえた。閂がゆっくりギシギシ外されるのが聞こえるのと同時に猿の手が見つかり、夫は夢中で三つ目の、最後の願いを口にした。

ノックはぴたっと止んだが、その谺は依然家のなかに漂っていた。椅子が引き戻されてドアが開くのを夫は聞いた。冷たい風が階段を駆け上がってきた。妻が長い、けたたましい、失意と悲嘆の叫び声を上げたのに力を得て夫は彼女のもとに駆け降りていき、そのまま木戸まで飛んでいった。向かいでちらちら光る街灯が、静かな人気のない道路を照らしていた。

ちなみに

「猿の手」は人気ユーモア作家だったジェイコブズが初めて書いた怪奇小説であり、編集者に送られた原稿には「ユーモアの種が尽きてしまって申し訳ない」と断り書きが添えてあった。編集者もこれまでのジェイコブズのイメージに合わないということでしばらく放置し、ほかの執筆者の原稿が間に合わなかったときに、まさに穴埋めとして「猿の手」を掲載した。1899 年 7 月に送られた原稿が日の目を見たのは、ようやく 1902 年 9 月のことだった。

The Lottery

Shirley Jackson

くじ

シャーリイ・ジャクスン

シャーリイ・ジャクスン
(Shirley Jackson, 1916-1965)

シンプルな文章でグロテスクな状況や共同体を巧みに描き、生前から大いに人気を博したアメリカの作家。死後半世紀以上経ったいまも、その評価はますます高まっているように思える。代表的長篇に *The Haunting of Hill House* (1959) があり、またここで取り上げた有名な "The Lottery" をはじめ短篇にも秀作が多い。

The morning of June 27th was clear and sunny, with the fresh warmth of a full-summer day; the flowers ❶were blossoming profusely and the grass was richly green. The people of the village began to gather in the square, between the post office and the bank, around ten o'clock; in some towns there were so many people that the lottery took two days and had to be started on June 26th, but in this village, where there were only about three hundred people, the whole lottery took less than two hours, so ❷it could begin at ten o'clock in the morning and still be through in time to allow the villagers to get home for ❸noon dinner.

The children assembled first, of course. ❹School was recently over for the summer, and the feeling of liberty ❺sat uneasily on most of them; they tended to gather together quietly for a while before they ❻broke into boisterous play, and their talk was still of the classroom and the teacher, of books and ❼reprimands. Bobby Martin had already ❽stuffed his pockets full of stones,

❶ were blossoming profusely: ふんだんに咲いていた、咲き乱れていた
❷ it could begin at ten o'clock in the morning and still be through in time to ...: 午前10時に始めて、それでも（still）～するのに間に合う時間に終われる。be through: 終わる
❸ noon dinner: 昼の食事。p. 38, l. 3と同じ。
❹ School was recently over for the summer: 学校は最近終わって夏休みになっていた
❺ sat uneasily on most of them: 直訳は「彼らの大半に落着かなげに載っていた」。
❻ broke into boisterous play: 騒々しく遊びはじめた。broke into <break into ...: 突然～しはじめる
❼ reprimand(s): 叱責

6月27日の朝は澄みわたった晴れの日で、夏の盛りの爽やかな暖かさに満ちていた。花は咲き乱れ、草はみずみずしく青い。村人たちは10時ごろから、郵便局と銀行のあいだにある広場に集まりはじめた。町によっては人口も多く、くじに2日かかるので、6月26日に始めないといけないところもあったが、この村は人の数も300程度なので、くじには2時間とかからず、午前10時に始めても村人たちが昼の食事に帰れる時間に終わるのだった。

むろんまずは子供たちが集まってきた。学校は夏休みに入ったばかりで、大半の子はまだ自由の気分になじんでおらず、騒々しい遊びを始める前にしばらく静かに固まっていることもしばしばで、話題にするのもまだ教室、先生、教科書、誰それが叱られたといった事柄だった。ボビー・マーティンはすでにポケットに一杯石を貯(た)めていて、ほかの子たちもじきそれに倣い、一

❽ stuffed his pockets full of stones: ポケットに石を一杯詰め込んだ

and the other boys soon followed his example, selecting the smoothest and roundest stones; Bobby and Harry Jones and Dickie Delacroix— ❶the villagers pronounced this name "Dellacroy"— eventually made a great pile of stones in one corner of the square and guarded it against the ❷raids of the other boys. The girls stood aside, talking among themselves, ❸looking over their shoulders at the boys, and the very small children rolled in the dust or clung to the hands of their older brothers or sisters.

Soon the men began to gather, surveying their own children, speaking of ❹planting and rain, tractors and taxes. They stood together, away from the pile of stones in the corner, and their jokes were quiet and they smiled rather than laughed. The women, wearing faded house dresses and sweaters, came shortly after their ❺menfolk. They greeted one another and exchanged bits of gossip as they went to join their husbands. Soon the women, standing by their husbands, began to call to their children, and the

❶ the villagers pronounced this name "Dellacroy": 村人たちはその名を「デラクロイ」と発音した。Delacroix はフランス系の名前であり、本来なら /də-la-kʀwɑ/ と発音されるべきだが、村人たちにそういう素養はない。非英語系の名前が英語的に発音されてしまうことはむろん珍しくない。第 2 巻 Stuart Dybek, "Farwell" の「ちなみに」(p. 22) を参照。

❷ raid(s):（不意の）襲撃

❸ looking over their shoulders at the boys: ちらちらうしろを向いて男の子たちを見て。over one's shoulders は「肩越しに」と訳されることも多いが、要するに、首から上だけ回してふり返っているということ。

❹ planting: 種まき、植え付け

❺ menfolk: 男連中

番滑らかで丸い石を選びはじめた。ボビー、ハリー・ジョーンズ、ディッキー・ドラクロワ――村人たちはその名を「デラクロイ」と発音したが――の３人がやがて広場の隅に大きな石の山を築き、ほかの男の子たちが襲ってこないよう警備についていた。女の子は脇に集まって自分たちだけで喋りながらチラチラ男の子の方をふり返り、小さな子供たちは埃の中を転がったり兄や姉の手にしがみついたりしていた。

じきに男たちも集まってきて、自分の子供の居所を確かめ、種まきや雨、トラクターや税金の話をした。彼らは隅の石の山から離れて一緒に立ち、静かに冗談を言いあって、笑うにしても黙って微笑むだけだった。女たちは色褪せた普段着やセーターを着て、男連中より少し遅れてやって来た。たがいに挨拶を交わし、噂話をやりとりしながらそれぞれ夫の許に向かっていく。まもなく、夫と並んで立った女たちが自分の子供を呼びはじめ、子供たちは

children came ❶reluctantly, having to be called four or five times. Bobby Martin ❷ducked under his mother's grasping hand and ran, laughing, back to the pile of stones. His father ❸spoke up sharply, and Bobby came quickly and took his place between his father and his oldest brother.

The lottery was ❹conducted— ❺as were the square dances, the teen-age club, the Halloween program—by Mr. Summers, who had time and energy to ❻devote to ❼civic activities. He was a round-faced, ❽jovial man and he ❾ran the coal business, and people were sorry for him, because he had no children and his wife was ❿a scold. When he arrived in the square, carrying the black wooden box, there was a murmur of conversation among the villagers, and he waved and called, "⓫Little late today, folks." ⓬The postmaster, Mr. Graves, followed him, carrying a three-legged stool, and the stool was put in the center of the square and Mr. Summers set the black box down on it. The villagers kept their distance, leaving a

❶ reluctantly: しぶしぶ
❷ duck(ed): ひょいと下げる
❸ spoke up: ここでは「声を張りあげた」という意味もあるが､speak up は「言うべきことをはっきり言う」「(沈黙のなかで) きちんと意見を表明する」というニュアンスを帯びることが多い。
❹ conduct(ed): ～を行なう、指揮する
❺ as were the square dances, ...: スクエアダンスや～などと同様に。square dance はアメリカ各地で踊られていた伝統的ダンス。
❻ devote to ...: devote A to B の形で、「A を B に注ぎ込む」の意となる (A は時間や金、労力など)。
❼ civic activities: 町や村の活動、催し
❽ jovial: 陽気な、快活な

四回、五回と呼ばれてしぶしぶやって来るのだった。ボビー・マーティンはつかまえようとする母親の手を逃れ、笑いながら石の山に駆け戻った。が、父親が厳しい声を上げるとすぐさま戻ってきて父と一番上の兄のあいだに立った。

村の活動に注ぐ時間も精力もある人物ということで、スクエアダンス、ティーンエイジクラブ、ハロウィーンの催しなどと同様、くじもサマーズ氏が指揮を執っていた。氏は丸顔の快活な人物で、石炭販売に携わり、子供はいないし妻はガミガミ屋とあって、人々は彼に同情していた。黒い木の箱を手にサマーズ氏が広場に現われると、村人たちのあいだに小声の会話が生じ、氏は手を振って「皆さん、今日は少し遅くなりました」と声を上げた。郵便局長のグレーヴズ氏が三本脚の丸椅子を持ってうしろに続き、丸椅子が広場の真ん中に置かれるとサマーズ氏が黒い箱をその上に置いた。村人たちは近

❾ ran <run: 〜を経営する
❿ a scold: ガミガミ女
⓫ Little late today: I'm a little late today. 以下、村人たちの発言は適宜語句を補って読む必要がある。
⓬ The postmaster: 郵便局長

space between themselves and the stool, and when Mr. Summers said, "❶Some of you fellows want to give me a hand?" ❷there was a hesitation before two men, Mr. Martin and his oldest son, Baxter, came forward to ❸hold the box steady on the stool while Mr. Summers ❹stirred up the papers inside it.

The original ❺paraphernalia for the lottery had been lost long ago, and the black box now resting on the stool had been put into use even before Old Man Warner, the oldest man in town, was born. Mr. Summers spoke frequently to the villagers about making a new box, but ❻no one liked to upset even as much tradition as was represented by the black box. There was a story that the present box had been made with some pieces of the box that had ❼preceded it, the one that had been ❽constructed when the first people settled down to make a village here. Every year, after the lottery, Mr. Summers began talking again about a new box, but every year ❾the subject was allowed to fade off without anything's

❶ Some of you fellows want to give me a hand?: Would some of you ...?
❷ there was a hesitation before ...: ～する前にためらいがあった＝ためらいが生じたが、やがて～した
❸ hold the box steady: 箱をしっかりと押さえている
❹ stirred up ...: ～をかき回した
❺ paraphernalia: 道具
❻ no one liked to upset even as much tradition as was represented by the black box: 直訳は「黒い箱によって体現されている程度の伝統さえ、誰もかき乱すことを好まなかった」。
❼ precede(d): ～に先行する
❽ construct(ed): ～を組み立てる
❾ the subject was allowed to fade off: 直訳は「その話題は立ち消えになるが

よりはせず、丸椅子から一定の距離を置いて、サマーズ氏が「何人か、手伝ってもらえますかな？」と言ったときもまずはためらったが、やがて男２人──マーティン氏とその長男バクスター──が歩み出て、サマーズ氏が中の紙をかき回すあいだ、丸椅子に載った箱をしっかり押さえていた。

くじに使う元来の道具はとうの昔に失われ、いま丸椅子の上に載っている黒い箱にしても、村一番の年長者ウォーナー老人が生まれるよりもっと前から使われていた。新しい箱を作ってはどうか、とサマーズ氏は何度も村人たちに持ちかけていたが、ささやかであれ黒い箱が体現している伝統を断ち切りたがる者は一人もいなかった。一説によれば、現在の箱はかつての、ここに村を作ろうと最初に人々が移住してきた際に作った箱の一部を使って作られたということだった。毎年くじが終わったあとにサマーズ氏が新しい箱の件を蒸し返しても、結局何もなされぬまま話は立ち消えになった。黒い箱は

ままにされた」。

being done. The black box grew ❶shabbier each year; by now it was no longer completely black but ❷splintered badly along one side to show the original wood color, and in some places faded or stained.

Mr. Martin and his oldest son, Baxter, held the black box securely on the stool until Mr. Summers had stirred the papers ❸thoroughly with his hand. Because so much of ❹the ritual had been forgotten or ❺discarded, Mr. Summers had been successful in ❻having slips of paper substituted for the chips of wood that had been used for generations. Chips of wood, Mr. Summers had argued, ❼had been all very well when the village was tiny, but ❽now that the population was more than three hundred and likely to keep on growing, it was necessary to use something that would fit more easily into the black box. The night before the lottery, Mr. Summers and Mr. Graves made up the slips of paper and put them into the box, and it was then taken to ❾the safe of Mr. Summers'

❶ shabbier <shabby: みすぼらしい
❷ splintered badly along one side: ある面はひどく裂けていて
❸ thoroughly: 徹底的に
❹ the ritual: 儀式
❺ discard(ed): ～を捨てる
❻ having slips of paper substituted for the chips of wood: 紙切れを木片の代わりに使わせる。substitute A for B: AをBの代わりに使う
❼ had been all very well >be all very well: ～で十分である（たいていそのあとにbutが来る）
❽ now that ...: ～しているいまとなっては
❾ the safe: 金庫

年々みすぼらしくなっていき、いまではもう完全に黒くはなく、ある面などはひどくささくれ立って元の木の色が露出していたし、何か所かは色褪せたりしみが付いたりしていた。

マーティン氏とその長男バクスターにしっかり押さえてもらい、サマーズ氏は片手で黒い箱の中の紙をよくかき混ぜた。儀式の大半はすでに忘れられるか捨てられるかしていたので、それまで何世代も使われていた木切れの代わりに紙切れを導入することにはサマーズ氏も成功していた。村がひどく小さかったころには木切れも結構だったろうが、人口が300を超えて今後ももっと増えそうだとなれば何かもっと箱に入れやすいものを使わないと、と氏は唱えたのである。くじの前の晩、サマーズ氏とグレーヴズ氏とで紙切れを用意して箱に入れたら、サマーズ氏の石炭販売会社の金庫に持っていき、

coal company and locked up until Mr. Summers was ready to take it to the square next morning. The rest of the year, the box was put away, sometimes one place, sometimes another; it had spent one year in Mr. Graves's barn and another year underfoot in the post office, and sometimes it was set on a shelf in the Martin grocery and left there.

❶There was a great deal of fussing to be done before Mr. Summers ❷declared the lottery open. There were the lists to make up—of ❸heads of families, ❹heads of households in each family, members of each household in each family. There was ❺the proper swearing-in of Mr. Summers by the postmaster, as ❻the official of the lottery; at one time, some people remembered, there had been ❼a recital of some sort, performed by the official of the lottery, ❽a perfunctory, tuneless chant that ❾had been rattled off duly each year; some people believed that the official of the lottery used to stand ❿just so when he said or sang it, others believed that he was

❶ There was a great deal of fussing to be done before ...: ～する前に多くの細かいことをやる必要があった。fuss(ing): （小さなことを）騒ぎ立てる
❷ declared the lottery open: くじの開始を宣言した
❸ heads of families: 家系の長
❹ heads of households in each family: それぞれの家系内の世帯の長
❺ the proper swearing-in: しかるべき就任宣誓。swearing-in <swear in ...: ～を就任宣誓させる
❻ the official of the lottery: くじの管理人、執行人
❼ a recital of some sort: ある種の朗誦（ろうしょう）
❽ a perfunctory, tuneless chant: おざなりの、節もろくにない文句
❾ had been rattled off duly: しかるべくすらすらと唱えられた。rattle off はほとんど考えずに言葉をくり出す感じ。

翌朝氏が広場へ持っていくまでしまっておく。この日以外は、箱は一年間、いろんな場所に保管された。ある年はグレーヴズ氏の家の納屋だったし、ある年は郵便局の床、また時にはマーティン食料雑貨店の棚の上に置かれたままのこともあった。

サマーズ氏がくじの開始を宣言するまでには、あれこれ手続きがあった。まずリストを作らねばならない。家系の長のリスト、それぞれの家系内の世帯の長のリスト、それぞれの家系内のそれぞれの世帯の構成員のリスト。それから、郵便局長がサマーズ氏をくじ執行人として正式に任命する。ひところはある種の朗誦(ろうしょう)のようなものがあったと一部の人々は記憶していて、節もないおざなりな文句をくじ執行人が毎年しかるべく吟じたということで、それを唱えるだか歌うだかする際に執行人があるポーズを取って立っていたと考える人もいれば、人々の中を歩き回ることになっていたと考える人もい

⑩just so: ぴったりの姿で。"in the required or appropriate manner" (*Oxford English Dictionary*)。

supposed to walk among the people, but years and years ago this part of the ritual had been allowed to ❶lapse. There had been, also, ❷a ritual salute, which the official of the lottery had had to use in ❸addressing each person who came up to draw from the box, but this also had changed with time, until now it was felt necessary only for the official to speak to each person approaching. Mr. Summers was very good at all this; in his clean white shirt and blue jeans, with one hand resting carelessly on the black box, he seemed very proper and important as he talked ❹interminably to Mr. Graves and the Martins.

Just as Mr. Summers finally ❺left off talking and turned to the assembled villagers, Mrs. Hutchinson came hurriedly along the path to the square, her sweater thrown over her shoulders, and ❻slid into place in the back of the crowd. "❼Clean forgot what day it was," she said to Mrs. Delacroix, who stood next to her, and they both laughed softly. "Thought ❽my old man was ❾out back

❶ lapse: 廃れる
❷ a ritual salute: 儀式的な挨拶の文句
❸ address(ing): ～に声をかける
❹ interminably: 果てしなく、だらだらと
❺ left off talking: 話すのをやめた
❻ slid into place: しかるべき場所に滑り込んだ。in place: 本来の場所に、適切な位置に
❼ Clean forgot: すっかり忘れていた
❽ my old man: うちの亭主
❾ out back stacking wood: 家の裏に出て薪を積んでいる

たが、もう何年も前にこの部分は省かれるようになっていた。また、くじを引きに歩み出た人物一人ひとりに執行人が声をかける際に使うべき決まり文句も以前にはあったが、これも時とともに変わって、いまではやって来る人それぞれに執行人が何か言葉をかければいいだけになっていた。こうしたことすべてにサマーズ氏は非常に長けていた。清潔な白いシャツにブルージーンズ姿で片手をさりげなく黒い箱に載せ、グレーヴズ氏とマーティン親子とひっきりなしに喋っている氏は、いかにもこの役に相応しい貫禄ある人物に見えた。

やっとお喋りを終えたサマーズ氏が、集まった村人たちの方に向き直ったところで、セーターを肩に羽織ったハッチンソン夫人が広場に至る小道をそそくさとやって来て群衆のうしろに滑り込んだ。「すっかり忘れてたよ、今日のこと」と彼女は隣にいるデラクロイ夫人に言い、二人は小声で笑った。「うちの亭主が裏で薪を積んでると思ってたんだけど」とハッチンソン夫人はさ

stacking wood," Mrs. Hutchinson went on, "and then I looked out the window and ❶the kids was gone, and then I remembered it was the twenty-seventh and ❷came a-running." She ❸dried her hands on her apron, and Mrs. Delacroix said, "You're in time, though. They're ❹still talking away up there."

Mrs. Hutchinson ❺craned her neck to see through the crowd and found her husband and children standing near the front. She tapped Mrs. Delacroix on the arm as a farewell and began to make her way through the crowd. The people ❻separated good-humoredly to let her through; two or three people said, ❼in voices just loud enough to be heard across the crowd, "Here comes ❽your Missus, Hutchinson," and "Bill, ❾she made it after all." Mrs. Hutchinson reached her husband, and Mr. Summers, who had been waiting, said cheerfully, "Thought we were going to have to ❿get on without you, Tessie." Mrs. Hutchinson said, grinning, "⓫Wouldn't have me leave m'dishes in the sink, now, would you,

❶ the kids was gone: the kids were gone でないところが庶民的な響き。p. 16, l. 16 などと同じ。

❷ came a-running: 走ってきた。a- が入るのは古めかしい響き。

❸ dried her hands on her apron: dried は「乾かした」ではなく「拭いた」。

❹ still talking away up there: あっちでまだ無駄口を叩いている。talk(ing) away: べらべら喋る。up there: あっちの方で（up は「あっち」が中心であることを示唆）

❺ craned her neck to see through the crowd: 人だかりの向こうまで見通そうと首をのばした

❻ separated good-humoredly to let her through: 彼女を通してやろうと愛想よく左右に分かれた

❼ in voices just loud enough to be heard across the crowd: 人だかりの向

らに言った。「ふっと窓の外を見たら子供たちがいなくなってて、ああそうだ今日は27日だって思い出して飛んできたんだよ」。夫人がエプロンで両手を拭くと、デラクロイ夫人が「まあでも間に合ったよ。あっちでまだぺちゃくちゃ喋ってるから」と言った。

ハッチンソン夫人が首をのばして人だかりを見渡すと、夫と子供たちが前の方に立っていた。彼女はデラクロイ夫人の腕をとんとん叩いて別れを告げ、人混みの中を進んでいった。人々は愛想よく道を空けて彼女を通してやった。二、三人が人だかり越しにかろうじて届く声で「かみさんが来たぜ、ハッチンソン」「ビル、奥さん間に合ったぜ」と呼びかけた。ハッチンソン夫人が夫の許に着くと、待っていたサマーズ氏が陽気に「あんた抜きでやる破目になるかと思ったよ、テシー」と言った。ハッチンソン夫人はニヤッと笑って「皿を流しに入れっぱなしにゃできないでしょ、ジョー？」と言い、ハッチンソ

こうまでどうにか届く大きさの声で
❽ your Missus: あんたのかみさん
❾ she made it after all:（間に合わないかと思ったが）間に合った
❿ get on without you: あんた抜きで進める
⓫ Wouldn't have me leave m'dishes in the sink, now, would you: 文頭に You を補う。直訳は「(あなたは) 私に食器を流しに入れっぱなしにはさせないでしょう？」。m'dishes: my dishes

Joe?," and soft laughter ran through the crowd as the people ❶stirred back into position after Mrs. Hutchinson's arrival.

"Well, now," Mr. Summers said ❷soberly, "guess we better get started, ❸get this over with, ❹so's we can go back to work. ❺Anybody ain't here?"

"Dunbar," several people said. "Dunbar, Dunbar."

Mr. Summers consulted his list. "Clyde Dunbar," he said. "That's right. ❻He's broke his leg, hasn't he? Who's drawing for him?"

"Me, I guess," a woman said, and Mr. Summers turned to look at her. "Wife draws for her husband," Mr. Summers said. "Don't you have a grown boy to do it for you, Janey?" Although Mr. Summers and everyone else in the village knew the answer perfectly well, it was the business of the official of the lottery to ask such questions formally. Mr. Summers waited with an expression of polite interest while Mrs. Dunbar answered.

❶ stirred back into position: ごそごそ動いて元の場所に戻った
❷ soberly: 真顔で、真面目な顔で
❸ get ... over with: ～をさっさと終わらせる。with のあとに何か語が来るのではない。
❹ so's we can go back to work: so that we can go back to work。so as to go back to work に引っぱられた、非標準的だがよく目にする言い方。
❺ Anybody ain't here?: Is there anybody who isn't here?（誰かここにいない人はいるか？）
❻ He's broke his leg: He's broken his leg

ン夫人の登場で乱れた人々の位置が元に戻るとともに静かな笑い声が人の輪を流れていった。

「さて、それでは始めるとしようか」とサマーズ氏が真顔で言った。「さっさと終わらせて、仕事に戻らんと。誰かいない者はおるかね？」

「ダンバー」と何人かが言った。「ダンバー、ダンバー」

サマーズ氏がリストを調べた。「クライド・ダンバー。その通りだ。たしか脚を折ったんじゃなかったかね？　誰が代わりに引く？」

「あたしだろうね」と一人の女が言い、サマーズ氏がそっちを向いて彼女を見た。「夫がいなければ妻が引く」と氏は言った。「あんた、代わりに引いてくれる大きい息子はおらんかね、ジェイニー？」。サマーズ氏にもほかの村人たちにも答えはわかりきっていたが、そうした質問を公式に発するのがくじ執行人の仕事なのである。礼儀正しい興味の表情を浮かべて待つサマーズ氏に向かって、ダンバー夫人は答えた。

"❶Horace's not but sixteen yet," Mrs. Dunbar said regretfully. ❷"Guess I gotta fill in for the old man this year."

"Right," Mr. Summers said. He made a note on the list he was holding. Then he asked, "Watson boy drawing this year?"

A tall boy in the crowd raised his hand. "Here," he said. "I'm drawing for ❸m'mother and me." He blinked his eyes nervously and ❹ducked his head as several voices in the crowd said things like "❺Good fellow, Jack," and "❻Glad to see your mother's got a man to do it."

"Well," Mr. Summers said, "❼guess that's everyone. Old Man Warner make it?"

"Here," a voice said, and Mr. Summers nodded.

❽A sudden hush fell on the crowd as Mr. Summers ❾cleared his throat and looked at the list. "All ready?" he called. "Now, I'll read the names—heads of families first—and the men come up and

❶ Horace's not but sixteen yet: Horace is only sixteen yet
❷ Guess I gotta fill in for the old man this year: I guess I have to fill in ...。fill in for ...: ～の代わりをする、穴を埋める
❸ m'mother: my mother
❹ ducked his head: 首をすくめた
❺ Good fellow, Jack: いいぞ、ジャック
❻ Glad to see your mother's got a man to do it: I'm glad to see your mother has a man to do the drawing
❼ guess that's everyone: これで全員だな
❽ A sudden hush: 突然の静寂
❾ cleared his throat: 咳払いした

「ホレスはまだ16だからねえ」とダンバー夫人は残念そうに答えた。「今年はまだあたしが亭主の代わりにやるっきゃありませんねえ」
「結構」とサマーズ氏は言って、手に持っているリストにメモを書き入れた。それから、「今年はワトソンの息子が引くのか？」と問いかけた。
人だかりの中ののっぽの若者が片手を上げた。「はい、母と僕を代表して僕が引きます」と若者は言った。彼が落着かなげに目をしばたたかせ首をすくめると、人だかりの中からいくつか「いいぞ、ジャック」「お前にやってもらってお袋さんも幸せだなあ」といった声が上がった。
「さて、ではみんな揃ったかな。ウォーナー爺さんは来てるか？」
「ここにいる」と声がして、サマーズ氏はうなずいた。

サマーズ氏がえへんと咳払いしてリストに目を落とすと、突然の静寂が群衆の上に降り立った。「みんな、いいか？」と氏は呼びかけた。「では、私が名前を、家長を最初に読み上げる。呼ばれた者たちは前に出て、箱から紙を

take a paper out of the box. Keep the paper folded in your hand without looking at it ❶until everyone has had a turn. Everything clear?"

The people had done it so many times that they only half listened to the directions; most of them were quiet, wetting their lips, not looking around. Then Mr. Summers raised one hand high and said, "Adams." A man ❷disengaged himself from the crowd and came forward. "Hi, Steve," Mr. Summers said, and Mr. Adams said, "Hi, Joe." They grinned at one another ❸humorlessly and nervously. Then Mr. Adams reached into the black box and took out a folded paper. He ❹held it firmly by one corner as he turned and went hastily back to his place in the crowd, where he stood a little apart from his family, not looking down at his hand.

"Allen," Mr. Summers said. "Anderson. . . . Bentham."

❺"Seems like there's no time at all between lotteries any more," Mrs. Delacroix said to Mrs. Graves in the back row. "Seems like we

❶ until everyone has had a turn: 全員がくじを引き終えるまで。a turn: 順番、機会

❷ disengaged himself from the crowd: 直訳は「自らを群衆から引き離した」。

❸ humorlessly: おもしろくもなさそうに

❹ held it firmly by one corner: 直訳は「それを隅でしっかり持った」。

❺ Seems like there's no time at all between lotteries any more: 直訳は「いまではもう、くじとくじとのあいだに全然時間がないように思える」。Seems like ...: It seems that ...

一枚引く。全員が引き終わるまで、紙は畳んだまま中は見ずに持っている。よろしいか？」

もうさんざんやってきたので、こうした指示をみんなろくに聞いていなかった。大半は周りも見ずに、黙って唇を濡らしている。それからサマーズ氏が片手を高く上げて「アダムズ」と言った。一人の男が人だかりから離れて歩み出てきた。「やあ、スティーヴ」とサマーズ氏は言い、アダムズ氏も「やあ、ジョー」と返した。二人はにっと、おかしくもなさげに、落着かなげに笑った。それからアダムズ氏が箱の中に手を入れ、畳んだ紙を取り出した。そして紙の端をしっかり握ったまま、回れ右して人の輪の中にそそくさと戻っていき、家族から少し離れて立った。手を見下ろしはしなかった。

「アレン」とサマーズ氏は言った。「アンダスン……ベンサム」

「最近はもう、くじからくじまであっという間だねえ」一番うしろの列でデラクロイ夫人がグレーヴズ夫人に言った。「つい先週、こないだのやつをやっ

❶got through with the last one only last week."

"❷Time sure goes fast," Mrs. Graves said.

"Clark. . . . Delacroix."

"❸There goes my old man," Mrs. Delacroix said. She held her breath while her husband went forward.

"Dunbar," Mr. Summers said, and Mrs. Dunbar went steadily to the box while one of the women said, "❹Go on, Janey," and another said, "There she goes."

"We're next," Mrs. Graves said. She watched while Mr. Graves ❺came around from the side of the box, greeted Mr. Summers gravely, and selected a slip of paper from the box. By now, all through the crowd there were men holding the small folded papers in their large hands, ❻turning them over and over nervously. Mrs. Dunbar and her two sons stood together, Mrs. Dunbar holding the slip of paper.

"Harburt. . . . Hutchinson."

❶ got through with <get through with ...: ～を終わらせる、片付ける
❷ Time sure goes fast: 時の経つのは本当に早い。sure は「正しく」は surely だが口語では sure も普通。
❸ There goes my old man: あそこにうちの亭主が行く＝うちの亭主の番だ
❹ Go on: 励ましの表現。「頑張れ」「行けぇ」といった感じ。
❺ came around from the side of the box: 箱の側面から回ってきた
❻ turning them over and over nervously: 何度も落着かなげにひっくり返して

た気がするよ」

「ほんとに早いねえ、時が経つのは」グレーヴズ夫人が言った。

「クラーク……デラクロイ」

「うちの旦那だ」デラクロイ夫人が言った。夫が歩み出るのを息をとめて見守っている。

「ダンバー」とサマーズ氏が言って、ダンバー夫人が確固とした足どりで箱に歩み出ると、女たちの一人が「頑張ってよ、ジェイニー」と言い、もう一人が「いよいよだね」と言った。

「次はうちだよ」とグレーヴズ夫人が言った。彼女が見守る前で、グレーヴズ氏が箱の側面から回ってきて、サマーズ氏に重々しく挨拶し、箱から紙切れをひとつ選んだ。いまではもう、人の輪のそこらじゅうで男たちが大きな手に小さな紙切れを持ち、落着かなげに何度もひっくり返している。ダンバー夫人は紙切れを手に息子二人と一緒に立っていた。

「ハーバート……ハッチンソン」

"❶Get up there, Bill," Mrs. Hutchinson said, and the people near her laughed.

"Jones."

"They do say," Mr. Adams said to Old Man Warner, who stood next to him, "that ❷over in the north village they're talking of giving up the lottery."

Old Man Warner ❸snorted. "❹Pack of crazy fools," he said. "❺Listening to the young folks, nothing's good enough for *them*. ❻Next thing you know, they'll be wanting to go back to living in caves, nobody work any more, ❼live *that* way for a while. ❽Used to be a saying about '❾Lottery in June, corn be heavy soon.' ❿First thing you know, we'd all be eating ⓫stewed chickweed and acorns. There's *always* been a lottery," he added ⓬petulantly. "⓭Bad enough to see young Joe Summers up there joking with everybody."

"Some places have already quit lotteries," Mrs. Adams said.

❶ Get up there: 行っておいで、がんばれ
❷ over in the north village: 北の村では。over が入って「あっちの方では」というニュアンスが強まる。
❸ snort(ed): 鼻を鳴らす
❹ (a) Pack of ...: ～の一味、群れ
❺ Listening to the young folks, nothing's good enough for them: 直訳は「若い連中の話を聞いていると、彼らにとって十分いいものは何もない」。標準的な文法からすれば、Listening の主語は nothing であるべき（二つの節の主語は一致すべき）だが、こういう破格は口語では普通。
❻ Next thing you know: 次はもう
❼ live that way for a while: しばらくそうやって暮らしてみろ
❽ Used to be a saying: There used to be a saying

「行ってきな、ビル」とハッチンソン夫人が言い、周りの人々が笑った。

「ジョーンズ」

「北の村じゃあ」とアダムズ氏が隣にいるウォーナー爺さんに言った。「くじをやめようっていう話が出てるそうですねえ」

ウォーナー爺さんはふんと鼻を鳴らした。「馬鹿どもが」と爺さんは言った。「若い奴らときたら、何から何までケチつけて。あれじゃじきに洞穴暮らしに戻ろうって言い出すぞ、もう誰も働かない暮らしに、そんな暮らしいっぺんやってみろってんだ。昔は『六月のくじ、実りは近い』といったもんだ。あの調子じゃみんな、ハコベとドングリ煮て食う破目になるぞ」。そして爺さんはさらに「くじはいつだってあったんだ」と拗(す)ねた口調で言い足した。「ジョー・サマーズの小僧があそこでみんなと冗談言いあって、それだけでも見ちゃおれんのに」

「もうすでにくじをやめた村もありますよね」とアダムズ夫人が言った。

❾ Lottery in June, corn be heavy soon: 六月にくじをやれば、じきにトウモロコシが重くなる（corn will be heavy soon)。格言らしく June と soon が韻を踏んでいる。
❿ First thing you know: 気がついたらもう
⓫ stewed chickweed and acorns: ハコベとドングリを煮たもの
⓬ petulantly: 拗ねたように、怒りっぽく
⓭ Bad enough to ...: ～するだけでも十分悪い

"❶Nothing but trouble in *that*," Old Man Warner said ❷stoutly. "Pack of young fools."

"Martin." And Bobby Martin watched his father go forward. "Overdyke. . . . Percy."

"I wish they'd hurry," Mrs. Dunbar said to her older son. "I wish they'd hurry."

"❸They're almost through," her son said.

"You get ready to ❹run tell Dad," Mrs. Dunbar said.

Mr. Summers called his own name and then stepped forward ❺precisely and selected a slip from the box. Then he called, "Warner."

"❻Seventy-seventh year I been in the lottery," Old Man Warner said as he went through the crowd. "Seventy-seventh time."

"Watson." The tall boy came awkwardly through the crowd. Someone said, "Don't be nervous, Jack," and Mr. Summers said, "❼Take your time, son."

❶ Nothing but trouble: 厄介以外何もない
❷ stoutly: 断固として
❸ They're almost through: もうほとんど終わった。p. 66, l. 9 の be through に同じ。
❹ run tell Dad: run and tell Dad
❺ precisely: 几帳面な様子で
❻ Seventy-seventh year I been in the lottery: This is the seventy-seventh year that I have been in the lottery
❼ Take your time: ゆっくりやれよ

「そんなことしたら厄介が起きるばかりだ」とウォーナー爺さんはきっぱり言った。「馬鹿な若僧どもが」

「マーティン」。父親が前に出るのをボビー・マーティンは見守った。「オーヴァーダイク……パーシー」

「さっさとやってくれないかねえ」ダンバー夫人が上の息子に言った。「さっさとやってほしいよ」

「もうじき終わりだよ」息子が言った。

「終わったらすぐ、父さんに知らせに行きな」ダンバー夫人が言った。

サマーズ氏が自分の名を呼んでつかつかと歩み出て、紙切れを一枚箱から選んだ。それから「ウォーナー」と呼び上げた。

「もうこれで77年目だよ」とウォーナー爺さんは人込みの中を進みながら言った。「77回目のくじだ」

「ワトソン」。のっぽの若者がぎこちなく人の輪から出てきた。「落着け、ジャック」と誰かが言い、サマーズ氏も「ゆっくりやれよ」と言った。

"Zanini."

After that, there was a long pause, ❶a breathless pause, until Mr. Summers, holding his slip of paper in the air, said, "All right, fellows." For a minute, no one moved, and then all the slips of paper were opened. Suddenly, all the women began to speak at once, saying, "Who is it?," "Who's got it?," "Is it the Dunbars?," "Is it the Watsons?" Then the voices began to say, "It's Hutchinson. It's Bill," "Bill Hutchinson's got it."

"Go tell your father," Mrs. Dunbar said to her older son.

People ❷began to look around to see the Hutchinsons. Bill Hutchinson was standing quiet, ❸staring down at the paper in his hand. Suddenly, Tessie Hutchinson shouted to Mr. Summers, "You didn't give him time enough to take any paper he wanted. I saw you. It wasn't fair!"

"❹Be a good sport, Tessie," Mrs. Delacroix called, and Mrs.

❶ a breathless pause: 息を殺した間

❷ began to look around:「〜はじめる」ということを英語は日本語より律儀に言うので、訳では省いてもいいと思えることも多い。

❸ staring down at the paper in his hand: 手に持った紙を呆然と見て。このstareにははっきり「驚き（と放心）」が感じられる。

❹ Be a good sport: まあいいじゃないか、白けることを言うなよ。a good sportは「状況を鷹揚に受け入れる人間」といった意。

「ザニーニ」

そのあと長い間が、息を殺した間があったのち、サマーズ氏が自分の紙切れを掲げて「よし、ではみんな」と言った。少しのあいだ誰も動かなかった。それから、すべての紙切れが一斉に開かれた。突然女たちが一気に喋り出した。「誰かしら？」「誰が当たったの？」「ダンバーさんのとこ？」「ワトソン一家かい？」。それからいくつかの声が「ハッチンソンだ。ビルだ」「ビル・ハッチンソンが当たった」と言った。

「父さんに知らせといで」ダンバー夫人が上の息子に言った。

人々はハッチンソン家の人々を探してあたりを見回した。ビル・ハッチンソンは静かに立って、手に持った紙を呆然と見下ろしていた。突然、テシー・ハッチンソンがサマーズ氏に向かって叫んだ。「あんた、ビルに選ぶ時間を十分くれなかったよ。あたしは見たんだ。フェアじゃなかったよ！」

「まあまあ、テシー」とデラクロイ夫人が呼びかけ、グレーヴズ夫人も「あ

Graves said, "All of us ❶took the same chance."

"Shut up, Tessie," Bill Hutchinson said.

"Well, everyone," Mr. Summers said, "that was done pretty fast, and now we've got to be hurrying a little more to ❷get done in time." He consulted his next list. "Bill," he said, "you draw for the Hutchinson family. You got any other households in the Hutchinsons?"

"There's Don and Eva," Mrs. Hutchinson yelled. "Make *them* take their chance!"

"Daughters draw with their husbands' families, Tessie," Mr. Summers said gently. "You know that as well as anyone else."

"It wasn't *fair*," Tessie said.

"❸I guess not, Joe," Bill Hutchinson said ❹regretfully. "My daughter draws with her husband's family, ❺that's only fair. And I've got no other family except the kids."

❶ took the same chance: 同じ危険を冒した。take a chance で「危険を冒す」「運に任せる」。

❷ get done in time: 時間内に終わらせる

❸ I guess not, Joe: ll. 6-7 の "You got any other households in the Hutchisons?"（ハッチンソン家にはほかにも世帯があるか）という問いへの答え。

❹ regretfully: 残念そうに

❺ that's only fair: それがフェアというものだ。公正なのだから仕方がない、という含み。彼はここで、妻がくり返す「フェアじゃなかった」という抗議をどれくらい意識しているだろうか？

たしたちみんな、同じ確率だったんだから」と言った。

「黙りなさい、テシー」とビル・ハッチンソンが言った。

「さて、皆さん」サマーズ氏が言った。「ここまでは割合早く済んだが、予定どおり終わらせるには、も少し急がなくちゃいけない」。氏は次のリストに目を落とした。「ビル」と氏は言った。「あんたがハッチンソンの家系を代表して引いたんだな。ハッチンソン家には、ほかに世帯があるかね？」

「ドンとエヴァがいるわよ」とハッチンソン夫人がわめいた。「あの二人にも引かせなさいよ！」

「娘は夫の家族の方で引くんだよ、テシー」サマーズ氏は穏やかに言った。「あんただってそれくらいわかってるだろう」

「フェアじゃなかったのよ」テシーは言った。

「いや、いないよ、ジョー」ビル・ハッチンソンは残念だという口調で答えた。「娘は亭主の家族の方で引く、それでフェアだ。そして俺は子供以外ほかに親族はいない」

"Then, ❶as far as drawing for families is concerned, it's you," Mr. Summers said in explanation, "and as far as drawing for households is concerned, that's you, too. Right?"

"Right," Bill Hutchinson said.

"How many kids, Bill?" Mr. Summers asked formally.

"Three," Bill Hutchinson said. "There's Bill, Jr., and Nancy, and little Dave. And Tessie and me."

"All right, then," Mr. Summers said. "Harry, you got ❷their tickets back?"

Mr. Graves nodded and held up the slips of paper. "Put them in the box, then," Mr. Summers directed. "Take Bill's and put it in."

"I think we ought to ❸start over," Mrs. Hutchinson said, as quietly as she could. "❹I tell you it wasn't *fair*. You didn't give him time enough to choose. ❺*Every*body saw that."

❶ as far as drawing for families is concerned: 家系を代表してくじを引くという限りでは
❷ their tickets: みんなが引いた紙切れのこと。
❸ start over: 最初からやり直す
❹ I tell you: 主張していることを強調する言い方。
❺ *Every*body saw that: ハッチンソン夫人の必死の口調をイタリクスで再現している。

「それでは、あんたは家系を代表して引いたのであり」とサマーズ氏は整理した。「所帯を代表して引いたのでもあると。そうだね？」

「そうだ」ビル・ハッチンソンは言った。

「子供は何人だね、ビル？」サマーズ氏は改まった口調で訊いた。

「三人」ビル・ハッチンソンは言った。「ビル・ジュニア、ナンシー、それにデイヴ坊や。あとはテシーと俺だ」

「結構、それでは」サマーズ氏が言った。「ハリー、この人たちの紙は集めたかね？」

グレーヴズ氏がうなずいて、紙切れの束を掲げた。「じゃあそいつを箱に戻してくれ」とサマーズ氏が指示した。「ビルのも受けとって、中に入れてくれ」

「はじめからやり直すべきだと思うわ」とハッチンソン夫人が精一杯静かな声で言った。「言ったでしょ、フェアじゃなかったのよ。あんたはビルに選ぶ時間を十分与えなかったのよ。みんな見てたわよ」

Mr. Graves had selected the five slips and put them in the box, and he ❶dropped all the papers but those onto the ground, where the breeze caught them and lifted them off.

"Listen, everybody," Mrs. Hutchinson was saying to the people around her.

"Ready, Bill?" Mr. Summers asked, and Bill Hutchinson, with one quick glance around at his wife and children, nodded.

"Remember," Mr. Summers said, "take the slips and keep them folded until each person has taken one. Harry, you help little Dave." Mr. Graves took the hand of the little boy, who came ❷willingly with him up to the box. "Take a paper out of the box, Davy," Mr. Summers said. Davy put his hand into the box and laughed. "Take just *one* paper," Mr. Summers said. "Harry, you hold it for him." Mr. Graves took the child's hand and removed the folded paper from ❸the tight fist and held it while little Dave stood next to him and looked up at him ❹wonderingly.

"Nancy next," Mr. Summers said. Nancy was twelve, and her school friends breathed heavily as she went forward, ❺switching

❶ dropped all the papers but those onto the ground: それ以外の紙は全部地面に捨てた。ここの but は except の意（接続詞ではなく前置詞）。
❷ willingly: 進んで、嫌がらずに
❸ the tight fist: しっかり握ったこぶし
❹ wonderingly: 不思議そうに
❺ switching her skirt: スカートをさっさっと揺らして

グレーヴズ氏は紙切れを5つ選んで箱に入れ、ほかの紙はみんな地面に捨てた。風がそれらを吹き上げて運び去った。

「みんな、聞いてよ」ハッチンソン夫人が周りの人々に言っていた。

「用意はいいか、ビル？」サマーズ氏が訊ね、妻と子供たちをチラッと一目見てからビル・ハッチンソンはうなずいた。

「忘れるなよ」サマーズ氏は言った。「紙切れを取ったら、全員が取るまで畳んだまま持っていること。ハリー、デイヴ坊やを手伝ってやってくれ」。グレーヴズ氏が小さな男の子の手を握ると、男の子は嫌がりもせず一緒に箱の前に来た。「紙をひとつ箱から取りなさい、デイヴィ」とサマーズ氏が言った。デイヴィは箱に手を入れてきゃっきゃっと笑った。「ひとつだけ取るんだよ」とサマーズ氏は言った。「ハリー、あんたが持っていてやってくれ」。グレーヴズ氏は子供の手を摑んで、きつく握ったこぶしから畳んだ紙切れを抜きとって自分で持ち、デイヴ坊やは隣に立ってよくわからないという顔でグレーヴズ氏を見上げた。

「次はナンシーだ」サマーズ氏が言った。12歳のナンシーがスカートをしゅっしゅっと揺すって前に出て上品な手付きで紙切れを一枚取るのを、学校の友人たちは息も荒く見守った。「ビル・ジュニア」とサマーズ氏が言い、赤ら

her skirt, and took a slip ❶daintily from the box. "Bill, Jr.," Mr. Summers said, and Billy, his face red and his feet overlarge, nearly knocked the box over as he got a paper out. "Tessie," Mr. Summers said. She hesitated for a minute, looking around ❷defiantly, and then ❸set her lips and went up to the box. She ❹snatched a paper out and held it behind her.

"Bill," Mr. Summers said, and Bill Hutchinson reached into the box and ❺felt around, bringing his hand out at last with the slip of paper in it.

The crowd was quiet. A girl whispered, "I hope it's not Nancy," and the sound of the whisper reached the edges of the crowd.

"❻It's not the way it used to be," Old Man Warner said clearly. "People ain't the way they used to be."

"All right," Mr. Summers said. "Open the papers. Harry, you open little Dave's."

❶ daintily: 優雅に、上品に
❷ defiantly: 挑むように
❸ set her lips: 唇をきっと結んだ
❹ snatched a paper out: 紙を一枚ひっつかんで出した
❺ felt around: 手探りした
❻ It's not the way it used to be: 昔とは違う

顔で足もやたら大きいビリーは紙を取り出す際に危うく箱を倒してしまうところだった。「テシー」サマーズ氏が言った。彼女はしばしためらい、挑むように周りを見回してから、きゅっと唇を結んで箱の前に出た。そして紙切れをひとつひっ摑み、うしろ手に持った。

「ビル」サマーズ氏が言い、ビル・ハッチンソンが箱に手を入れて中を探り、少ししてからようやく紙切れを摑んだ手を出した。

人の輪は静かだった。一人の女の子が「ナンシーじゃないといいけど」とささやき、そのささやき声が輪の端まで届いた。

「昔とは変わっちまった」ウォーナー爺さんがはっきりした声で言った。「人も昔とは変わっちまった」

「よし、それじゃ」サマーズ氏が言った。「紙を開きなさい。ハリー、デイヴ坊やのを開けてやってくれ」

Mr. Graves opened the slip of paper and ❶there was a general sigh through the crowd as he held it up and everyone could see that it was blank. Nancy and Bill, Jr., opened theirs at the same time, and both ❷beamed and laughed, turning around to the crowd and holding their slips of paper above their heads.

"Tessie," Mr. Summers said. There was a pause, and then Mr. Summers looked at Bill Hutchinson, and Bill unfolded his paper and showed it. It was blank.

"It's Tessie," Mr. Summers said, and his voice was hushed. "Show us her paper, Bill."

Bill Hutchinson went over to his wife and forced the slip of paper out of her hand. It had a black spot on it, the black spot Mr. Summers had made ❸the night before with the heavy pencil in the coal-company office. Bill Hutchinson held it up, and there was a stir in the crowd.

"All right, folks," Mr. Summers said. "Let's finish quickly."

❶ there was a general sigh: 直訳は「全員のため息があった」。
❷ beam(ed): 晴れやかにほほ笑む
❸ the night before: 前の晩に

グレーヴズ氏が紙切れを開けてそれを掲げ、何も印がないのを見てとると皆は一斉にため息を漏らした。ナンシーとビル・ジュニアは同時にそれぞれ開けて、二人とも目を輝かせ笑い声を上げながら人だかりの方を向き、紙切れを頭上にかざした。

「テシー」サマーズ氏が言った。間があって、それからサマーズ氏はビル・ハッチンソンを見て、ビルは紙を開いて、それを見せた。印はなかった。

「テシーだ」サマーズ氏が言った。ひどく静かな声だった。「テシーの紙を見せてくれ、ビル」

ビル・ハッチンソンは妻のところに行って、その手から紙切れを力ずくで奪った。紙には黒い点が描いてあった。前の晩に石炭販売会社の事務所でサマーズ氏が太い鉛筆を使って付けた印である。ビル・ハッチンソンがそれをかざし、群衆からざわめきが生じた。

「それじゃ皆さん」サマーズ氏が言った。「さっさと済ませましょう」

Although the villagers had forgotten the ritual and lost the original black box, they still remembered to use stones. The pile of stones the boys had made earlier was ready; there were stones on the ground with the blowing scraps of paper that had come out of the box. Mrs. Delacroix selected a stone so large she had to pick it up with both hands and turned to Mrs. Dunbar. "Come on," she said. "Hurry up."

Mrs. Dunbar had small stones in both hands, and she said, ❶gasping for breath. "I can't run at all. You'll have to ❷go ahead and I'll catch up with you."

The children had stones already, and someone gave little Davy Hutchinson a few pebbles.

Tessie Hutchinson was in the center of ❸a cleared space by now, and she held her hands out ❹desperately as the villagers ❺moved in on her. "It isn't fair," she said. A stone hit her on the side of the head.

❶ gasping for breath: 息を切らして、ゼイゼイ喘いで
❷ go ahead: 先に行く
❸ a cleared space: 空けられた空間
❹ desperately: 必死に
❺ moved in on her: 彼女に向かって迫っていった。テシーの周りの輪がどんどん閉じていく感じ。

儀式は忘れたし元の黒い箱も失くしていたが、人々は石を使うことは忘れていなかった。さっき男の子たちが作った石の山が待っていたし、紙切れが飛び交う地面にも石が転がっていた。デラクロイ夫人はものすごく大きな石を選んだので、両手を使って持ち上げねばならなかった。彼女はダンバー夫人の方を向いて「さあ、急ぐよ」と言った。

ダンバー夫人は小さな石を何個か両手で持ち、息をゼイゼイ言わせながら、「あたしゃ全然走れないよ。先に行っとくれ、あとから追いつくから」と言った。

子供たちはもう石を手にしていて、誰かがデイヴィ・ハッチンソンにも小石を何個か渡した。

いまやテシー・ハッチンソンは空けられた空間の真ん中に立ち、村人たちが迫ってくるなか、必死の形相で両手を突き出した。「フェアじゃないよ」と彼女は言った。石が一個、側頭部に当たった。

Old Man Warner was saying, "Come on, come on, everyone." Steve Adams was in the front of the crowd of villagers, with Mrs. Graves beside him.

"It isn't fair, it isn't right," Mrs. Hutchinson screamed, and then ❶they were upon her.

❶ they were upon her: 意図的にシンプルな表現が異様な生々しさを伝えている。

ウォーナー爺さんが「さあさあ、みんな」と言っていた。スティーヴ・アダムズは村人たちの先頭に立ち、かたわらにグレーヴズ夫人がいた。

「フェアじゃないよ、間違ってるよ」とハッチンソン夫人は金切り声を上げ、それからみんなは彼女に向かっていった。

ちなみに

この短篇が 1948 年 6 月 26 日の『ニューヨーカー』誌に掲載されると、その直後から罵倒・当惑・質問の手紙・電話が『ニューヨーカー』に殺到した。その大半は、現実と虚構の区別もろくにつけられない、まったくの無理解・誤解に基づく内容だった。電話はともかく、それらの手紙はすべて作者ジャクスンの許に送られ、のち 1960 年、その内容を紹介した講演原稿 “Biography of a Story”（ある短篇小説の伝記）をジャクスンは書いている。“I have all the letters still, and if they could be considered to give any accurate cross section of the reading public, or the reading public of *The New Yorker*, or even the reading public of one issue of *The New Yorker*, I would stop writing now.”（私はその手紙をまだ全部持っている。もしそれらが世の読者全体を正確に反映した見本と考えられるなら、あるいは『ニューヨーカー』誌の読者の、いや、『ニューヨーカー』特定の一号の読者の正確な見本だと考えられるだけでも、私はいますぐ書くのをやめるだろう。）

The Ones Who Walk Away from Omelas

(Variations on a theme by William James)

Ursula K. Le Guin

オメラスから歩き去る者たち

（ウィリアム・ジェームズの主題による変奏曲）

アーシュラ・K・ル＝グウィン

アーシュラ・K・ル＝グウィン
(Ursula K. Le Guin, 1929-2018)

『闇の左手』（*The Left Hand of Darkness*, 1969）、『所有せざる人々』（*The Dispossessed*, 1974）などのSF作品、「ゲド戦記」などのファンタジーで世界中に多くの読者を持つ作家。本作 “The Ones Who Walk Away from Omelas” は1973年に発表され、現在では短篇集 *The Unreal & the Real: Selected Short Stories Volume 2, Outer Space, Inner Lands* (2012) などに収録されている。

With ❶a clamor of bells that ❷set the swallows soaring, the Festival of Summer came to the city ❸Omelas, ❹bright-towered by the sea. ❺The rigging of the boats ❻in harbor sparkled with flags. In the streets between houses with red roofs and painted walls, between old ❼moss-grown gardens and under ❽avenues of trees, ❾past great parks and public buildings, ❿processions moved. Some were ⓫decorous: old people in long ⓬stiff robes of ⓭mauve and grey, ⓮grave master workmen, quiet, merry women carrying their babies and chatting as they walked. In other streets the music beat faster, a ⓯shimmering of gong and tambourine, and the people went dancing, the procession was a dance. Children ⓰dodged ⓱in and out, their ⓲high calls rising like the swallows' ⓳crossing flights over the music and the singing. All the processions ⓴wound towards the north side of the city, where on the great ㉑water-meadow called the Green Fields boys

⓿ 副題 Variations on a theme by William James: "Variations"（変奏曲）、"theme"（主題）は音楽用語。この副題の意味については「ちなみに」で述べるが、まずは小説を読むことをお薦めする。
❶ a clamor: 喧噪
❷ set the swallows soaring: 燕たちが空高く舞い上がるよう駆り立てた。set ... ～ing（…が～するようせき立てる）という定型句。
❸ Omelas: 作者本人によれば、発音は "O" に強勢がある。
❹ bright-towered: 明るい塔のある
❺ The rigging: 索具（船の帆やマストを支えるロープ・鎖類）
❻ in harbor: 停泊中で
❼ moss-grown: 苔の生えた
❽ avenues of trees: avenue はしばしば、街路樹のある通りを意味する。
❾ past:（空間的に）～を過ぎて、～の先に

鐘がけたたましく鳴って燕たちが舞い上がり、〈夏の祭〉がオメラスの街にやって来た。明るい塔の建つこの海辺の町で、港に停泊した一連のボートの索具には旗が飾られキラキラ光っている。街なかでは、屋根が赤く壁にはペンキを塗った家々のあいだ、苔むした古い庭と庭のあいだや道路脇に連なる並木の下、大きな公園や公共建築の向こう、といたるところで行列が動いていた。きちんと着飾った人もいる。藤色と灰色の長いこわばった式服を着た年配の人々、重々しい雰囲気の職人の親方、赤ん坊を抱えて歩きながらお喋りしている物静かで明るい女たち。通りによっては音楽もより速く鳴り、ゴングとタンバリンが光を浴びてゆらめき、人々は踊りに出てきた——行列自体が踊りなのだ。子供たちがひらひらと列から出入りし、彼らの甲高い呼び声が、交叉して飛び交う燕たちのように音楽や歌声と競いあって立ちのぼる。すべての行列はくねくね進んで街の北側に向かい、そちらにはグリーン・フィールズと呼ばれる広い湿地があって、まぶしい空気のなか裸になった男

❿ procession(s): 行列
⓫ decorous: 上品な、あらたまった
⓬ stiff robes: こわばった式服
⓭ mauve: 藤色の
⓮ grave master workmen: 重々しい様子の、職人の親方たち
⓯ shimmer(ing): ちらちら光る
⓰ dodge(d): ひらりと身をかわす
⓱ in and out: 出たり入ったり
⓲ high calls: 甲高い呼び声
⓳ crossing flights: 直訳すれば「交叉する飛翔」。
⓴ wound towards ...: 曲がりくねって〜の方に進んでいった。wound は wind /wáɪnd/ の過去形。
㉑ (a) water-meadow:（しばしば冠水する肥沃な）牧草地

and girls, naked in the bright air, with ❶mud-stained feet and ankles and long, ❷lithe arms, ❸exercised their restive horses before the race. The horses ❹wore no gear at all but a halter without bit. ❺Their manes were braided with streamers of silver, gold, and green. ❻They flared their nostrils and pranced and boasted to one another; they were vastly excited, ❼the horse being the only animal who has adopted our ceremonies as his own. ❽Far off to the north and west the mountains stood up ❾half encircling Omelas on her bay. The air of morning was so clear that the snow still ❿crowning the Eighteen Peaks ⓫burned with white-gold fire across the miles of sunlit air, under the dark blue of the sky. There was just enough wind to make the banners that marked the racecourse ⓬snap and flutter ⓭now and then. In the silence of the broad green meadows one could hear the music ⓮winding through the city streets, ⓯farther

❶ mud-stained: 泥で汚れた
❷ lithe: しなやかな
❸ exercised their restive horses: 進みたがらない馬たちを訓練した
❹ wore no gear at all but a halter without bit: 轡（くつわ）(bit) もない引き綱 (halter) 以外は何の引き具（gear）も着けていなかった
❺ Their manes were braided with streamers: たてがみ（manes）には飾りリボン（streamers）が編まれて (braided) いた
❻ They flared their nostrils and pranced and boasted to one another: 馬たちは鼻の穴（nostrils）を横に広げ（flared）、跳ねながら進み（pranced）、たがいに自慢しあった。flare their nostrils, prance といった語句は馬について一般的に使われるのに対し、boast はそれほど一般的ではないが、馬の誇らしげな様子が的確に伝わってくる。
❼ the horse being the only animal ...: Since the horse is the only animal ...
❽ Far off to the north: ずっと北の方に

の子女の子が、泥に汚れた足先とくるぶし、長いしなやかな腕を動かして、なかなか言うことを聞かぬ馬たちをレースに向けて訓練している。馬たちは轡（くつわ）もない端綱（はづな）以外は何の馬具も着けていない。たてがみには銀、金、緑のリボンが飾られている。鼻孔を広げ、跳ねて馬たちは進み、馬同士たがいに自慢しあっている。どの馬もひどく興奮していた。何しろ馬は、我々人間の行なう儀式を自分たちのものとして受け容れた唯一の動物なのだ。はるか北と西には山並みがそびえ、湾に面したオメラスを半ば囲んでいる。朝の空気はしんと澄みわたり、十八連山（エイティーン・ピークス）の頂をいまだ飾っている雪も、ダークブルーの空の下、白金（しろがね）色の炎に包まれて、何マイルも続く陽を浴びた空気の中を貫いていた。風はちょうど、馬の競走路を標（しる）す旗が時おりばさっと翻ってはためく程度に吹いている。広々とした緑の草地の静寂のなか、音楽がくねくねと街なかを進んでいくのが聞こえ、遠くなったり近くなったりしながらじわじ

❾ half encircling Omelas on her bay: 湾に面しているオメラスを半分囲むようにして

❿ crown(ing): ～のてっぺんを覆う

⓫ burned with white-gold fire: burned も fire も普通雪について使う言葉ではないが、雪がぎらぎら光っている様子がよく伝わってくる表現。

⓬ snap and flutter: 旗の動きを言っていて、snap はバサッと大きく揺れる感じ、flutter はパタパタと小さくはためく感じ。

⓭ now and then: 時おり

⓮ winding through the city streets: 都市の街路をくねくねと進んで。wind(ing) は p. 112, l. 14 の wound と同じ。

⓯ farther and nearer and ever approaching: 遠ざかったり（farther）近寄ったり（nearer）するが、大きな流れとしてはつねに（ever）近づいてくるということ。

and nearer and ever approaching, ❶a cheerful faint sweetness of the air that from time to time trembled and gathered together and ❷broke out into the great joyous clanging of the bells.

Joyous! How is one to tell about joy? How describe the citizens of Omelas?

They were not simple folk, you see, though they were happy. ❸But we do not say the words of cheer much any more. All smiles have become archaic. Given a description such as this ❹one tends to make certain assumptions. Given a description such as this one tends to look next for the King, ❺mounted on a splendid stallion and surrounded by his noble knights, or perhaps in ❻a golden litter borne by great-muscled slaves. But there was no king. They did not use swords, or keep slaves. They were not ❼barbarians. I do not know the rules and laws of their society, but I suspect that they were ❽singularly few. As they ❾did without monarchy and slavery, so they also ❿got on without ⓫the stock exchange,

❶ a cheerful faint sweetness of the air: 直訳は「空気の（空気中にある）明るい、かすかな甘美さ（さわやかさ）」。

❷ broke out into the great joyous clanging of the bells: 直訳は「一気に、大いなる、喜びあふれる鐘の轟きとなってほとばしり出た」。broke out into ... は *She broke out into laughter.*（わっと笑い出した）などと同じ。

❸ But we do not say the words of cheer much any more: だが私たちはもはや悦びの言葉をあまり言わない。突然 we が出てきて、オメラスの民（they）と対比される。次文の All smiles have become archaic.（笑顔はすべて古風なものになってしまった）もオメラスではなく「私たち」の世界のことである。archaic smile といえば、「初期ギリシア彫像の顔にみられる微笑に似た表情」（『リーダーズ英和辞典』）のことだが、ここではその古風な美しさより硬直ぶりが念頭に置かれている。

❹ one tends to make certain assumptions:（そういう説明を聞くと）人は

わ寄ってきて、空気をさわやかな快活さでほのかに染めるその音が、時おりぶるっと震えてはひとつにまとまり、大きな悦ばしい、けたたましい鐘の響きとなるのだった。

悦ばしい！　悦びというものをどう語ればいいのか？　オメラスの住民をどう語ればよいだろう？

彼らは幸福ではあったけれども、決して単純素朴な民ではなかった。一方我々はもはや、陽気な言葉をあまり口にしない。笑顔はすべて、古風で型にはまったものとなっている。オメラスの民をこんな風に言うと、きっとある種の臆測を誰もが持つだろう。こんなふうに言うと次は、王はどこだ、立派な雄馬に乗って気高い騎士たちに囲まれた、あるいは筋肉隆々の奴隷たちが担ぐ金色の輿で運ばれる王は、と誰もが探しはじめるだろう。だがオメラスには王などいない。人々は剣も使わなければ奴隷も所有しなかった。彼らは野蛮人ではなかった。その社会の決まり事や法律について私は知らないが、その数は著しく少なかったのではないかと思う。君主制も奴隷制もないのみならず、株式取引所も、広告も秘密警察も、核兵器もなしで彼らは暮らし

ある種の臆測をしがちである。one tends to ...（「人は〜しがちだ」）は we tend to ... でもほとんど変わらないが、この前後でオメラスの社会／一般社会の対比に we が使われていることもあり、one が自然な選択。

❺ mounted on a splendid stallion: 立派な雄馬に乗って

❻ a golden litter borne by great-muscled slaves: 筋肉隆々の奴隷たちによって運ばれる金色の輿。borne は bear（運ぶ）の過去分詞。

❼ barbarian(s): 野蛮人

❽ singularly few: 際立って少ない

❾ did without monarchy and slavery: 君主制、奴隷制なしで済ませていた

❿ got on without ...: すぐ前の did without とほぼ同じ。

⓫ the stock exchange: 株式取引所。要するに株というものが存在しなかったということ。

the advertisement, the secret police, and ❶the bomb. Yet I repeat that these were not simple folk, not ❷dulcet shepherds, noble savages, bland utopians. ❸They were not less complex than us. The trouble is that we have a bad habit, encouraged by ❹pedants and sophisticates, of considering happiness as something rather stupid. ❺Only pain is intellectual, only evil interesting. This is ❻the treason of the artist: a refusal to admit the ❼banality of evil and the terrible boredom of pain. ❽If you can't lick 'em, join 'em. If it hurts, repeat it. But to praise despair is to ❾condemn delight, to embrace violence is to ❿lose hold of everything else. We have almost lost hold; we can no longer describe a happy man, nor make any celebration of joy. How can I tell you about the people of Omelas? They were not naïve and happy children—though their children were, in fact, happy. They were ⓫mature, intelligent, passionate adults whose lives were not ⓬wretched. O miracle!

❶ the bomb: the が付いていて単数なので、単に「爆弾」ということではなく、「究極の爆弾」＝原水爆、核兵器を指す。

❷ dulcet shepherds, noble savages, bland utopians: 目に快い羊飼い、高貴な野蛮人、退屈なユートピア住民。どれもありきたりのイメージを皮肉って言っている。特に noble savages はルソーなどが広めた観念で、いわゆる「蛮人」はヨーロッパ文明に毒されておらず人間としての徳を失っていない、というロマンチックな信念に基づく。

❸ They were not less complex than us: 彼らが我々ほど複雑でないということはなかった。They were as complex as us と言うのに較べて、「単純だと思うかもしれないが、そんなことはない」という含みがある。

❹ pedants and sophisticates: 学者ぶる人間やすれっからしの人間

❺ Only pain is intellectual, only evil interesting: 痛みだけが知的であり、悪だけが興味深い。これは語り手の意見ではなく、前文で言っている我々の「悪し

ていた。だがもう一度言うが彼らは単純素朴な民ではなかった。心和む羊飼いでも、高貴な野蛮人でも、空疎なユートピア夢想家でもなかった。私たちに較べて複雑さが劣る、などということはなかったのである。問題は私たちが、学者ぶる連中や世慣れたすれっからしにそそのかされて、幸福というものを何やら愚かしいものと見る悪習に陥っていることだ。知的なのは苦痛のみであり、知的興味をそそるのは悪のみ。これは芸術家による裏切りである。悪の凡庸さ、苦痛の底なしの退屈さを連中は認めない。強いものには巻かれろ。痛ければ、もっとやれ。だが絶望を賛美するのは歓楽を排除することであり、暴力を称揚するのはほかのあらゆるものとのつながりをなくしてしまうことだ。私たちはいまやほとんどそのつながりをなくしかけている。幸福な人間というものを私たちはもはや言い表わせないし、悦びを褒めたたえることもできない。ならば私に、オメラスの人々をどうやって語れよう？　彼らは初心(うぶ)で幸福な子供たちではなかった（もっとも彼らの子供たちは事実幸福だったが）。彼らは成熟した、知的な、情熱的な、人生が無残になってしまっていない大人たちだった。おお、奇跡！　だがもっと上手く言い表わす

き習慣」の中身。

❻ the treason: 叛逆、裏切り

❼ banality: 陳腐さ。"the banality of evil" はアイヒマン裁判を記録したハンナ・アーレントの著書の副題として知られる（*Eichmann in Jerusalem: A Report on the Banality of Evil*）。

❽ If you can't lick 'em, join 'em: 奴らを負かすことができないなら奴らの仲間になれ＝長いものには巻かれろ。lick が beat になることもある。'em は them だがこのフレーズでは 'em になることが多い。

❾ condemn delight: 悦びを非難する、否定する。condemn はその前の praise の反対、delight は despair の反対。

❿ lose hold of everything else: ほかすべてのものを失ってしまう

⓫ mature: 成熟した

⓬ wretched: 惨めな、辛い

but I wish I could describe it better. I wish I could ❶convince you. Omelas sounds in my words like a city in a fairy tale, ❷long ago and far away, once upon a time. Perhaps it would be best ❸if you imagined it as your own fancy bids, assuming it will ❹rise to the occasion, for certainly I cannot ❺suit you all. For instance, how about technology? I think that there would be no cars or helicopters ❻in and above the streets; ❼this follows from the fact that the people of Omelas are happy people. Happiness is based on ❽a just discrimination of what is necessary, what is neither necessary nor destructive, and what is destructive. In the middle category, however—that of the unnecessary but undestructive, that of ❾comfort, luxury, exuberance, etc.— ❿they could perfectly well have central heating, subway trains, washing machines, and all kinds of marvelous devices not yet invented here, floating light-sources, fuelless power, a cure for the common cold. Or they could have none of that: it doesn't matter. ⓫As you like it. ⓬I incline to

❶ convince: ～を納得させる、説得する
❷ long ago and far away, once upon a time: 遠い過去の遠い国で、昔むかし。どちらもおとぎ話の出だしの決まり文句。
❸ if you imagined it as your own fancy bids: ご自分の空想（fancy）が命じる（bids）ままに想像すれば
❹ rise to the occasion: チャレンジングな状況で実力を発揮する、という意味の成句。
❺ suit: ～の気に入る、満足させる
❻ in and above the streets: in は cars について、above は helicopters について言っている。
❼ this follows from the fact that ...: ～という事実から、当然この結果になる
❽ a just discrimination: 正当な区別。just は形容詞。

力が私にあったら。あなた方を納得させる力があったら。私の語るオメラスは、まるでおとぎ話の中の街みたいに聞こえる。ずっと以前の、はるか遠い、昔々の街。おそらく最善なのは、あなた方に自分の空想の赴くままにオメラスを想像してもらうことではないか。あなた方の空想がその任に相応(ふさわ)しく働いてくれることを期待しよう。私一人であなた方みんなを満足させるのはとうてい無理な相談なのだから。たとえば、テクノロジーについてはどうか。街路に自動車はなく上空にヘリコプターもないと私は思う。これはオメラスの人々が幸福な人々だという事実から必然的に生じる。幸福とは、何が必要で、何は必要でも破壊的でもなく、何は破壊的かを正しく区別する力に基づいている。二番目のカテゴリー、すなわち不要だが非破壊的な、安楽・贅沢・華美等々に属す範疇に関しては、セントラルヒーティング、地下鉄、洗濯機、その他まだここでは発明されていないさまざまな装置を彼らが持っていていっこうに構わない。宙に浮かぶ光源、燃料なしの動力、風邪の特効薬。あるいは逆にそれらのどれひとつとして持っていないということでもいい。どちらでも構わないのだ。お好きなように。私としては、祭りの前のここ数

❾ comfort, luxury, exuberance: 安楽、贅沢、あふれる豊かさ。だんだん「豊か度」が上がっていく。
❿ they could perfectly well have ...: 〜を持っていても全然おかしくない
⓫ As you like it: お好きなように。同名のシェークスピアの戯曲邦題は、坪内逍遥以来、日本では一貫して「お気に召すまま」。
⓬ I incline to think that ...: 私としては〜だと考えたいと思う

think that people from ❶towns up and down the coast have been coming in to Omelas during the last days before the Festival on very fast little trains and ❷double-decked trams, and that the train station of Omelas is actually the handsomest building in town, though ❸plainer than ❹the magnificent Farmers' Market. But ❺even granted trains, I fear that ❻Omelas so far strikes some of you as goody-goody. Smiles, bells, parades, horses, ❼bleh. If so, please add ❽an orgy. ❾If an orgy would help, don't hesitate. Let us not, however, have temples from which issue beautiful nude ❿priests and priestesses already half in ecstasy and ready to ⓫copulate with any man or woman, lover or stranger, who ⓬desires union with the deep godhead of the blood, although that was my first idea. But really it would be better not to have any temples in Omelas—at least, not ⓭manned temples. Religion yes, ⓮clergy no. Surely the beautiful nudes can just ⓯wander about, offering themselves like

❶ towns up and down the coast: 沿岸一帯にあるあまたの町
❷ double-decked trams: 二階建ての路面電車
❸ plain(er): 簡素な、質素な
❹ the magnificent Farmers' Market: 壮大なファーマーズ・マーケット。現実でも、元来の「農民市場」は屋外だっただろうが、今日ではところによってはかなり立派な建物が建てられたりもしている。
❺ even granted ...: ～は認めるとしても
❻ Omelas so far strikes some of you as goody-goody: 直訳は「これまで語ったオメラスは、あなたたちの何人かには、善人ぶった感じに思える」。so far は「いままでのところ」、strike A as B で「B だという印象を A に与える」。
❼ bleh: グェ、ゲゲゲ。嫌悪の表現。
❽ an orgy: 飲めや歌えの大騒ぎ。乱交も示唆され、goody-goody の対極というイメージ。

日に沿岸のあちこちに点在する町からオメラスにやって来た人々が、超高速の小さな列車や二階建ての路面電車に乗ってきたのだと考えたいし、オメラスの鉄道駅が、まあファーマーズマーケットの壮観には劣るとしても建造物としては町で一番だと思いたい。が、鉄道があることは認めたとしても、こうしてこれまで語ったオメラスが、一部の人々には、善人ぶった連中の寄り集まりだろう、と思えてしまうことを私は恐れる。笑顔、鐘、パレード、馬……ゲゲゲ。もしそうだったら、そこに狂乱の宴も加えてほしい。狂乱の宴で足しになるなら、どうか躊躇しないでいただきたい。だがしかし、神殿から美しい裸の男祭司女祭司が出てきてもうすでに半ば恍惚に耽(ひた)っていて男であれ女であれ愛人であれ赤の他人であれ深遠なる血の神との合一を望む者誰とでも交合する気になっている、なんていうのはやめておこう（実のところ私がまず思いついたのはそういう情景だったのだが)。いや本当に、オメラスにはいかなる神殿もない方がいい——少なくとも人間のいる神殿は。宗教はよい、だが聖職者はいけない。美しき裸体の人があたりをさまよっていて、

❾ If an orgy would help, don't hesitate: orgy で足しになるのであれば、迷わず（あなたのオメラス像に）つけ加えてほしい
❿ priests and priestesses: 男女の司祭
⓫ copulate: 性交する
⓬ desires union with the deep godhead of the blood: 深遠な血の神との合体を望む。orgy という言葉から出てくるありきたりのイメージをさらに膨らませている。
⓭ manned: 人を配した、有人の
⓮ clergy: 聖職者
⓯ wander about: ぶらぶらさまよう

divine ❶souffles to ❷the hunger of the needy and the rapture of the flesh. Let them join the processions. Let tambourines be struck above the copulations, and the glory of desire be ❸proclaimed upon the gongs, and (a not unimportant point) let the ❹offspring of these delightful rituals be beloved and looked after by all. ❺One thing I know there is none of in Omelas is ❻guilt. But ❼what else should there be? I thought at first there were not drugs, but that is ❽puritanical. For those who like it, the faint insistent sweetness of ❾*drooz* may ❿perfume the ways of the city, *drooz* which first brings a great lightness and brilliance to the mind and ⓫limbs, and then after some hours a dreamy ⓬languor, and wonderful visions at last of ⓭the very arcana and inmost secrets of the Universe, as well as exciting the pleasure of sex beyond belief; and it is not ⓮habit-forming. For more modest tastes I think there ought to be beer. What else, what else belongs in the joyous city? The sense of

❶ souffle(s): スフレ。フランス語としては soufflé が正しいが、諸外国語の単語に付いているもろもろのアクセント記号に関し、英語圏の人々は概して無神経である。

❷ the hunger of the needy and the rapture of the flesh: 飢えたる者の渇望と、肉体の歓喜。依然として陳腐なイメージを膨らませている。

❸ proclaim(ed): ～を宣言する

❹ offspring: 結果として生じたもの、子孫

❺ One thing I know there is none of in Omelas: 直訳は「オメラスにまったくないと私が知っているひとつのもの」。I know there is none of ... in Omelas.（オメラスには～がまったくないと私は知っている）というセンテンスを想定するとわかりやすいか。

❻ guilt: 罪悪感

❼ what else should there be?: ほかに何が（オメラスにまったくないものとして）あるべきだろうか？

神々しいスフレのごとく、飢えた者たちにその身を差し出し、肉体の愉楽を与えている、これはむろん構わない。どんどん行列に加わってもらっていい。性交の上でタンバリンを鳴らすがいい、欲望の栄光がゴングによって宣言されるがいい、そして（この点もけっこう重要である）こうした悦ばしき儀式から生まれた者たちが、皆に愛され世話されるがいい。オメラスにこれだけはまったくない、と私にわかっているのは、罪悪感である。ならばほかにはどうか？　はじめ、麻薬はなし、と考えたのだが、それは厳格すぎるというべきだろう。お好みとあらば、ドゥルーズのかすかな、だが執拗な芳香が都市の暮らしに満ちるがいい。ドゥルーズはまず、精神と身体に大いなる軽さと輝かしさを与え、その数時間後、夢にも似た気だるさを生じさせ、最後に、宇宙をめぐるこの上なく深遠にして奥義なる秘密の素晴らしいビジョンがもたらされ、ついでに信じがたいほどの性的快楽が誘発される。しかも中毒性はない。もう少し穏やかなものを望む人のためにビールもあるべきだろう。ほかに何が、この悦びに満ちた街にはほかに何があるだろう？　勝利の感覚、

❽ puritanical: 清教徒的な、過度に厳格な
❾ *drooz*: 架空の麻薬の名として、意図的に安っぽい響きのものを選んだ観がある。
❿ perfume the ways of the city: 都市の暮らしに芳香を添える。the ways of the world という言い方はよく使われ、「世のやり方」「世の倣わし」といった意味。
⓫ limb(s): 手足
⓬ (a) languor: 気だるさ
⓭ the very arcana and inmost secrets of the Universe: 明らかに arcana and inmost で形容詞二つとして使われ、「秘密の、深奥の」といった意味だろうが、厳密に言えば arcana は「秘密」「奥義」の意の名詞であり、形容詞として正しいのは arcane。たしかに arcana の方が「奥義っぽい」響きが強いので、「気持ちはわかる」のだが。
⓮ habit-forming: 常用癖をもたらす、習慣性の

victory, surely, the celebration of courage. But as we did without clergy, let us do without soldiers. The joy built upon successful ❶slaughter is not the right kind of joy; ❷it will not do; it is fearful and it is ❸trivial. ❹A boundless and generous contentment, a ❺magnanimous triumph felt not against some outer enemy but ❻in communion with the finest and fairest in the souls of all men everywhere and the splendor of the world's summer: this is what ❼swells the hearts of the people of Omelas, and the victory they celebrate is that of life. I really don't think many of them need to take *drooz*.

Most of the procession have reached the Green Fields by now. A marvelous smell of cooking ❽goes forth from the red and blue tents of ❾the provisioners. The faces of small children are ❿amiably sticky; in the ⓫benign grey beard of a man a couple of ⓬crumbs of rich pastry ⓭are entangled. The youths and girls have mounted their horses and are beginning to group around the starting line

❶ slaughter: 大量殺人、殺戮（さつりく）
❷ it will not do: それでは駄目だ。will do / will not do の形で、「～でいい、間に合う／～では駄目だ、よくない」の意になる。"*When is it convenient for you?*" "*Any weekend will do.*"（「いつがご都合よろしいですか」「週末ならいつでも結構です」『コンパスローズ英和辞典』）
❸ trivial: 些細な、卑小な
❹ A boundless and generous contentment: 無限にして鷹揚な、満ち足りた気持ち
❺ magnanimous: 度量の大きい、心の広い
❻ in communion with ...: ～との交わりで
❼ swell(s): ～を膨らませる、満たす
❽ goes forth from ...: ～から出てくる

勇気の称揚、これは間違いない。だが聖職者をなしにしたのだから兵士もなしにしよう。殺戮（さつりく）の完遂に基づく悦びは、正しい種類の悦びではない。そういうのは恐ろしいばかりで、矮小であり、よくない。無限の広がりを有する大らかな満足、誰か外の敵に対してではなくあらゆるところにいるすべての人間の魂と世界の夏の壮麗さとの中の最良にして最高に美しい部分との交わりにおいて感じる気高い勝利感——これこそがオメラスの人々の心を満たすのであり、彼らが祝う勝利は生の勝利だ。彼らの中にドゥルーズの服用を必要とする人が大勢いるとは思えない。

行列の大半はすでにグリーン・フィールズに到着した。赤と青の食糧テントから料理の素晴らしい匂いが漂い出てくる。小さな子供たちの顔は可愛くべたつき、一人の男の柔和な白髪のあごひげにはこってりしたペストリーのかけらが二つばかり絡まっている。若い男女は馬にまたがり、競走場のスタートラインに集まってきている。小柄で太った、声を上げて笑っている老いた

❾ the provisioner(s): 食糧係。provisions で食糧、蓄えの意。
❿ amiably sticky: 直訳は「可愛らしくべたべたな」
⓫ benign: 温和な
⓬ crumb(s):（パンなどの）かけら、屑
⓭ are entangled: 絡まっている

of the course. An old woman, small, fat, and laughing, ❶is passing out flowers from a basket, and tall young men wear her flowers in their shining hair. A child of nine or ten sits at the edge of the crowd, alone, playing on a wooden flute. People pause to listen, and they smile, but they do not speak to him, for he never ceases playing and never sees them, his dark eyes wholly ❷rapt in the sweet, thin magic of the tune.

He finishes, and slowly lowers his hands holding the wooden flute.

As if ❸that little private silence were the signal, all at once a trumpet sounds from the pavilion near the starting line: ❹imperious, melancholy, piercing. The horses ❺rear on their slender legs, and some of them ❻neigh in answer. ❼Sober-faced, the young riders stroke the horses' necks and ❽soothe them, whispering, "Quiet, quiet, there my beauty, my hope. . . ." They begin to ❾form in rank along the starting line. The crowds along

❶ is passing out flowers: 花を配っている
❷ rapt in ...: 〜に熱中して
❸ that little private silence: そのささやかな、一人きりの沈黙。ひっそり笛を吹いていた子どもが吹くのをやめて生じた静寂をこう形容している。
❹ imperious, melancholy, piercing: 尊大で、憂鬱で、耳をつんざくような。通り一遍の音ではないことを印象づける形容詞三つの選択。
❺ rear:（馬が）後ろ足で立つ
❻ neigh: いななく
❼ Sober-faced: 神妙な顔をした。sober は drunk と対比すれば「酒を飲んでいない、しらふの」ということだが、もっと広く、静かに醒めた感じを表わすことが多い。
❽ soothe: 〜をなだめる、落ちつかせる

女性がバスケットから花を配り、背の高い若者たちが輝く髪にそれを飾る。九つか十の男の子が一人、人の群れの端に一人で座って木の笛を吹いている。人々は立ちどまって耳を澄まし、ニッコリ笑うが、子供に話しかけはしない。子供は一時(いっとき)も吹くのをやめず、彼らのことが目に入ってもいないからだ。その黒い瞳は、メロディの快い、淡い魔法に浸りきっている。

子供は吹き終え、木の笛を持った両手をゆっくりと下ろす。

あたかもそのひそやかな静寂が合図であったかのように、突如スタートラインのそばのパビリオンからトランペットの音(ね)が響く。有無を言わせぬ、憂いを帯びた、耳をつんざく音に、馬たちはほっそりした後ろ足で立ち上がり、何頭かは音に応えてヒヒンと鳴く。神妙な顔の若き騎手たちが馬の首を撫でてなだめ、「静かに、静かに、僕の麗しい馬、僕の希望……」とささやく。スタートラインに沿って彼らは一列に並びはじめる。競走場沿いに並ぶ人の群れは、

❾ form in rank: 列を作る

the racecourse are like a field of grass and flowers in the wind. The Festival of Summer has begun.

Do you believe? Do you accept the festival, the city, the joy? No? Then let me describe one more thing.

In a basement under one of the beautiful public buildings of Omelas, or perhaps in ❶the cellar of one of its ❷spacious private homes, there is a room. It has one locked door, and no window. A little light ❸seeps in dustily between cracks in the boards, ❹secondhand from a cobwebbed window somewhere across the cellar. In one corner of the little room a couple of mops, with ❺stiff, clotted, foul-smelling heads, stand near a ❻rusty bucket. The floor is dirt, a little damp to the touch, as cellar dirt usually is. The room is about three ❼paces long and two wide: ❽a mere broom closet or ❾disused tool room. In the room a child is sitting. It could be a boy or a girl. ❿It looks about six, but actually is nearly ten. It is ⓫feeble-minded. Perhaps it was born ⓬defective, or perhaps it has become

❶ the cellar: 地下
❷ spacious: 広々とした
❸ seeps in dustily between cracks in the boards: 直訳は「板のすきまから埃っぽくしみ込んでくる」。
❹ secondhand from a cobwebbed window: 直訳は「蜘蛛の巣が張った窓を通った中古の」。この一文で、光が入ってくることはくるのだが、それがいかにも冴えない、弱々しい光であることが印象づけられる。
❺ stiff, clotted, foul-smelling heads: 硬い、固まった、嫌な臭いのする頭部。モップ頭部の描写として実に的確な形容。
❻ rusty: 錆びた
❼ pace(s): 歩、歩幅
❽ a mere broom closet: 単なる掃除道具入れ。broom は「箒」。

風に吹かれる野原一面の草花のようだ。〈夏の祭り〉が始まったのだ。

あなたは信じるか？　この祭りを、街を、喜びを受け容れるか？　ノー？　ならばもうひとつだけ説明させてほしい。

オメラスの美しい公共建築のどれかの地階に、あるいは広々とした個人宅のどれかの地下に、ひとつの部屋がある。鍵がかかったドアがひとつあって、窓はない。かすかな埃っぽい光が板のすきまから入ってくるが、それは地下室のどこかにある蜘蛛の巣の張った窓を通ってきた中古の光だ。小さな部屋の隅にモップが二本、固まってこわばり悪臭を放つ頭部を上にして、錆びたバケツのかたわらに立っている。床は土間で、地下の土間の常として触ると少し湿っている。部屋は縦三歩分、横二歩分の広さで、単なる掃除具入れ、使わなくなった工具置場という観がある。その部屋に、一人の子供が座り込んでいる。男の子かもしれないし、女の子かもしれない。6歳くらいに見えるが、実はもう10歳近い。子供は知恵の発育が遅れている。生まれつき障

❾ disused: 使われなくなった
❿ It looks about six, but actually is nearly ten: 以下、この子供には一貫して it という代名詞が使われる。子供について it を使うのは間違いではないが、現代ではほとんど使われず、使うと子供を非人間的に捉えているように響く。ここではまさにそれを意図している。
⓫ feeble-minded: 精神薄弱の
⓬ defective: 欠陥のある

❶imbecile through fear, ❷malnutrition, and neglect. It ❸picks its nose and occasionally ❹fumbles vaguely with its toes or ❺genitals, as it ❻sits hunched in the corner farthest from the bucket and the two mops. It is afraid of the mops. It finds them horrible. It shuts its eyes, but it knows the mops are still standing there; and the door is locked; and nobody will come. The door is always locked; and nobody ever comes, except that sometimes—the child has no understanding of time or interval—sometimes the door ❼rattles terribly and opens, and a person, or several people, are there. One of them may come in and kick the child to make it stand up. The others never come close, but ❽peer in at it with frightened, disgusted eyes. The food bowl and ❾the water jug are hastily filled, the door is locked, the eyes disappear. The people at the door never say anything, but the child, who has not always lived in the tool room, and can remember sunlight and its mother's voice, sometimes speaks. "I will be good," it says. "Please let me out. I

❶ imbecile: 低能の
❷ malnutrition, and neglect: 栄養不足と、世話不足
❸ picks its nose: 鼻をほじる
❹ fumbles vaguely: 漠然ともてあそぶ
❺ genitals: 生殖器
❻ sits hunched: 背中を丸めて座っている
❼ rattles terribly: ガタガタ騒々しく鳴る
❽ peer in at it with frightened, disgusted eys: 怯えた、嫌悪した目で子供の方を覗き込む
❾ the water jug: 水差し

がいを抱えていたのかもしれないし、恐怖、栄養不足、放置のせいで知能が損なわれてしまったのかもしれない。子供は鼻をほじくり、時おり足指か性器をもてあそびながら、バケツとモップ二本から一番遠い隅にうずくまっている。子供はモップを怖がっている。モップを恐ろしいと思っている。子供は目を閉じるが、モップ二本がまだそこに立っていることを知っている。ドアには鍵がかかっていて、誰も来ることはない。ドアにはつねに鍵がかかっていて、誰も来ないが、ただ時おり——子供には時間とか間隔といった観念もない——時おりドアがガタガタ鳴って開き、誰かが一人、あるいは数人、そこにいる。うち一人が入ってきて、子供を立たせようと蹴飛ばすこともある。ほかの者たちは絶対に寄ってこず、怯えと嫌悪が入り混じった目をすぼめて子供をじっと覗き見ている。食べ物のボウルと水差しが急いで満たされ、ドアに鍵がかけられ、一連の目が消える。ドアのところに来た人たちは決して何も言わないが、子供はずっとこの工具置場で暮らしてきたわけではなく陽の光も母の声も思い出せるので、時おり言葉を発する。「いい子にするから」

will be good!" They never answer. The child used to scream for help at night, and cry a good deal, but now it only makes a kind of ❶whining, "eh-haa, eh-haa," and it speaks less and less often. It is so thin there are no ❷calves to its legs; its belly ❸protrudes; it lives on a half-bowl of ❹corn meal and grease a day. It is naked. Its ❺buttocks and thighs are ❻a mass of festered sores, as it sits in its own ❼excrement continually.

They all know it is there, all the people of Omelas. Some of them have come to see it, others are content merely to know it is there. They all know that it has to be there. Some of them understand why, and some do not, but they all understand that their happiness, the beauty of their city, the tenderness of their friendships, the health of their children, the wisdom of their scholars, ❽the skill of their makers, even ❾the abundance of their harvest and ❿the kindly weathers of their skies, depend wholly on this child's ⓫abominable misery.

❶ whining <whine: 幼児や犬が上げる哀れっぽい声や、大人の愚痴っぽい声などを表わす語。
❷ calves: ふくらはぎ（calf の複数形）
❸ protrude(s): 突き出る
❹ corn meal and grease: ひき割りトウモロコシ粉と、油脂
❺ buttocks: 尻
❻ a mass of festered sores: 大量のただれた腫れ物
❼ excrement: 排泄物
❽ the skill of their makers: 彼らの街の職人たちの技術
❾ the abundance of their harvest: 彼らの畑の収穫の豊富さ
❿ the kindly weathers of their skies: 彼らの空の温和な天候
⓫ abominable: おぞましい

と子供は言う。「お願いだから出して。いい子にするから！」。人々は決して答えない。子供はかつては夜になると助けを求めて金切り声を上げ、さんざん泣いたが、いまではもう哀れっぽい「エー＝ハァ、エー＝ハァ」という音を立てるだけで、喋ることもだんだん減ってきた。すっかり痩せこけて、脚からはふくらはぎがまったくなくなっている。お腹は突き出ている。毎日コーンミールと獣脂をボウル半分食べて生きている。服は着ていない。尻と腿は常時自分の汚物にまみれて座り込んでいるせいで爛れた腫れ物の巣だ。

子供がそこにいることを彼らはみな知っている。オメラスの住民全員が知っているのだ。子供を見に来たことのある者もいれば、単にそこにいるとわかっているだけで満足している者もいる。子供がそこにいなくてはいけないことを彼らはみな知っている。なぜなのか理解している者も理解していない者もいるが、自分たちの幸福、自分たちの街の美しさ、自分たちの友人関係の優しさ、自分の子供たちの健康、学者たちの叡智、職人たちの技術、さらには豊富な収穫、晴れた温和な空さえも、この子供の忌まわしいみじめさに全面的に依存していることを彼らはみな理解している。

This is usually explained to children when they are between eight and twelve, whenever they seem capable of understanding; and most of those who come to see the child are young people, though often enough an adult comes, or comes back, to see the child. No matter how well the matter has been explained to them, these young ❶spectators are always shocked and ❷sickened at the sight. They feel disgust, ❸which they had thought themselves superior to. They feel anger, ❹outrage, impotence, ❺despite all the explanations. They would like to do something for the child. But there is nothing they can do. ❻If the child were brought up into the sunlight out of that ❼vile place, if it were cleaned and fed and comforted, that would be a good thing indeed; but if it were done, in that day and hour all ❽the prosperity and beauty and delight of Omelas would ❾wither and be destroyed. Those are ❿the terms. ⓫To exchange all the goodness and grace of every life in Omelas

❶ spectator(s): 見物人
❷ sicken(ed): 〜に吐き気を催させる
❸ which they had thought themselves superior to: 直訳は「自分たちがそんなものは超越していると思っていたところの」。
❹ outrage, impotence: 憤り、無力感
❺ despite all the explanations: すべての説明にもかかわらず＝どれだけちゃんと説明されても
❻ If the child were brought up into the sunlight: もし子供が、日の光ある地上に連れていかれたら。この be brought up は「育てられる」ではなく文字どおり「上に連れていかれる」。
❼ vile: ひどい、忌まわしい
❽ the prosperity: 繁栄

これは子供たちには、8歳から12歳のあいだの、もう理解できそうだと思えた時点で説明され、子供を見に来る者たちも大半は若い世代である。とはいえ大人も相当数見に来るし、中には前にも来てまた戻ってくる大人もいる。どれだけきちんと説明してもらっていても、若き見物人たちは子供を見てかならずショックを受けゾッとする。自分はそんなものを感じるほど非情ではないと思っていたような嫌悪を彼らは子供に対して感じる。いくら説明されても、怒りを、憤りを、無力感を感じる。子供のために何かしてやりたいと彼らは思う。だができることは何もない。もし子供がその呪わしい場所から陽光の下に連れ出してもらったら、もし子供が体を綺麗にしてもらい食べ物を与えられ安楽にしてもらったらもちろん素晴らしいだろうがそうなったら、まさにその日その時間に、オメラスの繁栄と美しさと悦ばしいものはすべて衰え、消滅する。それが条件なのだ。そのただひとつのささやかな改善を得るには、オメラスのすべての生のあらゆる有難さ素晴らしさを引換えに差し出さねばならない。一人の幸福を求めるためには数千人の幸福を捨て

❾ wither: 弱る、衰える
❿ the terms: 条件
⓫ To exchange all the goodness ... for that single ...: exchange A for B（AをBと交換する）という形。goodness and grace: よさ、素晴らしさ

for that single, small improvement: to throw away the happiness of thousands for ❶the chance of the happiness of one: ❷that would be to let guilt within the walls indeed.

The terms are strict and absolute; ❸there may not even be a kind word spoken to the child.

Often the young people go home in tears, or in a tearless rage, when they have seen the child and ❹faced this terrible paradox. They may ❺brood over it for weeks or years. But as time goes on they begin to realize that even if the child could be ❻released, it ❼would not get much good of its freedom: a little vague pleasure of warmth and food, no doubt, but little more. It is too ❽degraded and imbecile to know any real joy. It ❾has been afraid too long ever to be free of fear. Its habits are too ❿uncouth for it to respond to ⓫humane treatment. ⓬Indeed, after so long it ⓭would probably

❶ the chance of the happiness of one: 一人が幸せになるチャンス。つまり万人の幸福を捨てても、引き換えに一人が幸福になると決まっているわけではない。

❷ that would be to let guilt within the walls indeed: それこそまさに（indeed）罪悪感を街の中に入れることになるだろう。p. 124, ll. 5-6 でオメラスにはguiltがまったくない、と言ったことを踏まえている。the walls とあるのは、中世の町が壁によって閉ざされていたことに基づく。

❸ there may not even be a kind word spoken to the child: 子供に向けてひとことの優しい言葉さえ発してはならない

❹ faced this terrible paradox: この恐ろしいジレンマに直面して。paradox は、この場合もそうだが、いわゆる論理的な「逆説」「二律背反」という意味になるとは限らず、こちらを立てればあちらが立たぬ、といった「板挟み」「ジレンマ」程度の意味になることも多い。

❺ brood over it: そのことについてじっと考え込む

ないといけない。そうなれば一気に罪悪感が街を囲む壁の中に入ってくるだろう。

条件は厳密であり絶対的である。子供に優しい言葉一言をかけてもいけない。

子供を目にし、この恐ろしい板挟みに直面した若き世代の者たちは、しばしば涙ぐんで、あるいは涙なき憤怒に包まれて帰っていく。このことについて、数週間、数年考え込む者もいる。だが時が経つにつれて彼らにもだんだんわかってくる。もしかりに解放してやれたとしても、あの子供にとって自由は大して足しになるまい。まあたしかに、暖かさと食べ物がもたらす若干の漠たる快楽はあるだろう。だがそれだけだ。あそこまで退化し、知能が損なわれてしまっては、真の悦びなど知りようもない。あまりに長いこと恐怖に包まれてきたせいで、怖いという気持ちから解き放たれることはもはやあるまい。あそこまでひどい習慣に浸ってしまったいま、人間らしい扱いに反応することもできないだろう。実際、もう慣れきってしまったせいで、もし

❻ release(d): ～を解放する、自由にする
❼ would not get much good of its freedom: その自由から大した善は得ないだろう＝自由になってもあまり得るものはないだろう
❽ degraded: 退化した
❾ has been afraid too long ever to be free of fear: あまりに長いあいだ恐れてきたので、今後恐怖から自由になることはありえない。ever はこのような否定的な文脈で使われれば要するに never の意を示唆する。したがってここでは、自由になることが永久にない、という響き。
❿ uncouth: 粗野な
⓫ humane: 人間らしい
⓬ Indeed: 実際、それどころか
⓭ would probably be wretched without walls about it: 自分の周りに（about it）壁がなかったらたぶん辛い思いをするだろう。about は around と同義。

be wretched without walls about it to protect it, and darkness for its eyes, and its own excrement to sit in. ❶Their tears at the bitter injustice dry when they begin to perceive ❷the terrible justice of reality, and to accept it. Yet it is their tears and anger, the trying of their generosity and ❸the acceptance of their helplessness, which are perhaps the true source of the ❹splendor of their lives. ❺Theirs is no vapid, irresponsible happiness. They know that they, like the child, are not free. They know ❻compassion. It is the existence of the child, and their knowledge of its existence, that makes possible the ❼nobility of their architecture, the ❽poignancy of their music, the ❾profundity of their science. It is because of the child that they are so gentle with children. They know that if the wretched one were not there ❿sniveling in the dark, the other one, the flute-player, could make no joyful music as the young riders line up in their beauty for the race in the sunlight of the first morning of summer.

❶ Their tears at the bitter injustice dry when ...: ～するとき、むごい不正に対する涙は乾く。dry は動詞。

❷ the terrible justice: 恐ろしい公正。the bitter injustice との対比（というより通底か)。

❸ the acceptance of their helplessness: 自分が無力だと認めること

❹ splendor: 壮麗さ

❺ Theirs is no vapid, irresponsible happiness: 彼らの幸福は、気の抜けた無責任な幸福などではない。Their happiness is ... と言わずに Theirs is ... と始めるのはやや格好をつけた言い方。*But stand close by Bette Davis, because hers was such a lonely life.*（でもベティ・デイヴィスには寄りそってあげてほしい　とても寂しい一生だったから。The Kinks, "Celluloid Heroes" の歌詞の一節）

身を護ってくれる壁もなくなり、目を包んでくれる闇も、座具代わりの自らの排泄物もなくなったら、たぶんひどく惨めな思いに陥るにちがいない。むごい不正に涙していた彼らが、現実の恐ろしい公正さを認識しはじめ、それを受け容れはじめると、涙も乾いてゆく。とはいえ、彼らの涙と怒り、己の優しさに対する試練、己の無力感の受け容れ、それこそがおそらく、彼らの人生の壮麗さの真の源なのだ。彼らの幸福とは、気の抜けた無責任な幸福では決してない。自分も子供と同じく自由ではないことを彼らは知っている。同情というものを彼らは知っている。あの子供が存在すること、子供が存在することを自分たちが知っていることこそが、気高い建築、切実な音楽、深遠な科学を可能にしている。あの子供がいるおかげで彼らはほかの子供たちにかくも優しくなれる。あのみじめな子が闇の中でメソメソ泣いていなかったら、もう一人の子供、笛を吹く子供が、夏の始まる朝の陽光のもと若き騎手たちが美しい姿で並ぶなか、悦ばしい音楽を奏でられもしないことを彼らは知っている。

❻ compassion: 同情、思いやり
❼ nobility: 気高さ
❽ poignancy: 痛ましさ、切実さ
❾ profundity: 深遠さ
❿ snivel(ing): メソメソする、哀れっぽく泣く

❶Now do you believe in them? ❷Are they not more credible? But there is one more thing to tell, and this is quite ❸incredible.

❹At times one of the ❺adolescent girls or boys who go to see the child does not go home to weep or rage, does not, ❻in fact, go home at all. Sometimes also a man or woman much older ❼falls silent for a day or two, and then leaves home. These people go out into the street, and ❽walk down the street alone. They keep walking, and ❾walk straight out of the city of Omelas, ❿through the beautiful gates. They keep walking across the farmlands of Omelas. Each one goes alone, youth or girl, man or woman. Night falls; the traveler must pass down village streets, between the houses with yellow-lit windows, and on out into the darkness of the fields. Each alone, they go west or north, towards the mountains. They go on. They leave Omelas, they walk ahead into the darkness, and they do not come back. ⓫The place they go towards is a place even less imaginable to most of us than the city of happiness. I cannot

❶ Now do you believe in them?: これであなたも彼らに believe in するだろうか？　この believe in は単に「〜の存在を信じる」という意味ではなく、「〜の存在意義を、正しさを信じる」ということ。*The people want a President they can believe in.*（国民は「この人ならいい」と思える大統領を求めている。*Longman Dictionary of Contemporary English*）

❷ Are they not more credible?: いまや彼らは、より信じられる存在になっていないだろうか？

❸ incredible: 信じがたい。前行の credible との対比をはっきり意識して使っている。

❹ At times: 時おり

❺ adolescent: 思春期の

❻ in fact: それどころか、そもそも

これであなたも彼らの存在を受け容れられるだろうか？　これで彼らもだいぶ信じられる存在になったのではないか？　だが語るべきことはもうひとつあり、これはおよそ信じがたい。

時おり、子供を見に行った思春期の女の子男の子の一人が、涙や怒りに包まれて家に帰らないことが、そもそもまったく家に帰らないことがある。また時にはもっとずっと年上の男か女が一日か二日黙り込んだのち、家から出ていくことがある。これらの人々は街路に出ていき、一人で歩いていく。歩きつづけて、そのまま美しい門を抜けてオメラスの街の外まで歩いていく。街の外の農地を彼らは歩いていく。少年であれ少女であれ、大人の男であれ女であれ、それぞれが一人で歩く。夜になり、旅人は村の道を通っていかねばならない。窓に黄色い明かりの灯った家々のあいだを過ぎ、野原の闇の中へ入っていく。それぞれが一人で、西か北へ行き、山へ向かう。彼らは進みつづける。オメラスを去り、目の前に広がる闇の中へ歩いていき、戻ってこない。彼らが向かう場所は、私たちの大半にとって、幸福の街以上に想像しがたい場所だ。私にはとうてい言葉にできない。そんな場所は存在しないと

❼ falls silent: 黙り込む

❽ walk down the street: 通りを歩いていく。down は中心から離れていくという含み。坂道を下るということではない。

❾ walk straight out of the city of Omelas: オメラスの街からそのまま歩いて出ていく

❿ through the beautiful gates: 美しい門を抜けて。p. 138, l. 3 で出てきた街を囲む壁（the walls）は一応比喩だったが、この gates は物語の中の現実である。やはりオメラスにはどこか中世的な雰囲気が漂う。

⓫ The place they go towards: 彼らが行こうとして向かっている場所。the place they go to との違いは、to だと the place がはっきり「到達点」という感じだが、towards だとあくまで「目標点」（たどり着くかどうかはわからない）という含み。

describe it at all. It is possible that it does not exist. But they seem to know where they are going, the ones who walk away from Omelas.

いう可能性もある。だが彼らは、オメラスから歩き去る者たちは、自分がどこへ向かっているか知っているように見える。

ちなみに

作品の副題に示されているとおり、この短篇の着想は哲学者ウィリアム・ジェームズの論文 “The Moral Philosopher and the Moral Life” (1891) 中の一節に基づいている。ジェームズはそこで、要約すれば「数百万人の恒久的な幸福が、一人の哀れな人間が孤独な責め苦の生を送ることを条件としていると聞いたら、誰もがまず一瞬、その幸福にしがみつこうと思うかもしれないが、その後ただちに感じるのは、そのような取引の結果として生まれる幸福とはなんとおぞましいものか、という思いではないか」と問いかけている。

また、Omelasという「地名」は、道路を車で走っていて、バックミラーに “Salem, Oregon”(オレゴン州セーレム)という道路標識が映ったのを見たことから生まれたと作者は述べている。

The Junky's Christmas

William Burroughs

ジャンキーのクリスマス

ウィリアム・バロウズ

★★☆

ウィリアム・バロウズ
(William Burroughs, 1914-1997)

1950年代の反抗する若き芸術家集団「ビート・ジェネレーション」を代表する詩人がアレン・ギンズバーグだとすれば、バロウズは小説家の筆頭格である。ウィリアム・テルごっこをして妻を射殺してしまったり、私生活でのスキャンダルも多く、存命中から神格化された人物だった。文章をバラバラに刻んでランダムにつなげる「カットアップ」の手法で知られ、主要作品は難解なところも多いが、1989年発表の*Interzone*に収録されたこの短篇は、拍子抜けするほどわかりやすい人情話である。

It was Christmas Day and Danny ❶the Car Wiper ❷hit the street ❸junk-sick and broke after seventy-two hours in ❹the precinct jail. It was a clear bright day, but there was no warmth in the sun. Danny ❺shivered with an inner cold. He ❻turned up the collar of ❼his worn, greasy black overcoat.

❽*This beat benny* ❾*wouldn't pawn for a deuce,* he thought.

❿He was in the West Nineties. A long block of ⓫brownstone rooming houses. Here and there ⓬a holy wreath in a clean black window. Danny's ⓭senses ⓮registered everything sharp and clear, with the ⓯painful intensity of junk sickness. The light hurt his ⓰dilated eyes.

He walked past a car, ⓱darting his pale blue eyes sideways ⓲in quick appraisal. There was a package on the seat and one of ⓳the ventilator windows was unlocked. Danny walked on ten

❶ the Car Wiper: べつにこういう職業があるわけではなく、人の車を拭いたりして小銭をもらい、隙あらば盗めるものは盗む人間ということ。
❷ hit the street: 街に出た
❸ junk-sick: クスリ切れで苦しい状態を言う。
❹ the precinct jail: precinct は警察小説などでは「〜分署」と訳される。
❺ shivered with an inner cold: 直訳は「内なる寒さに震えた」。
❻ turned up the collar: 襟を立てた
❼ his worn, greasy black overcoat: 着古した、垢じみた黒いコート
❽ *This beat benny*: このおんぼろのコート（benny はスラング）
❾ *wouldn't pawn for a deuce*: 質に入れたら２ドルにもならない。a deuce:（スラング）２ドル
❿ He was in the West Nineties: 西90丁目台にいた。この書き方で、ニューヨークを舞台にした小説だと見当がつく。マンハッタンで南北のおおよその位置を示すには、このように、東西にのびた通り（streets）を十単位で、さらに東側・

その日はクリスマスだった。車拭きのダニーは警察の留置場での72時間を終えて、薬が切れた一文なしの身で街に出た。晴れた明るい日だったが、陽には少しの暖かさもなかった。体の芯に寒気を抱えて、ダニーはぶるっと身震いした。着古しの、脂で汚れた黒いコートの襟を立てた。

こんなボロのコートじゃ質に入れても２ドルがせいぜいだな、とダニーは思った。

ここは西90丁目台。ブラウンストーン造りの下宿屋が何軒も、角から角まで並んでいる。あちこちの綺麗な黒い窓に、聖なる花輪が飾ってある。ダニーの五感は何もかもを、薬切れ固有の、痛いほどの強烈さで感じとった。瞳孔が開いた目に光が痛かった。

車が一台駐まっている。通りすぎながら、薄青い目をさっと横に向けて様子を見た。座席に何か包みが置いてあり、三角窓が片方ロックされていない。ダニーは３メートル歩きつづけた。あたりには誰もいない。指をぱちんと鳴

西側に分けて言うのが一般的。

⓫ brownstone rooming houses: ブラウンストーン作りの下宿屋。brownstone（褐色砂岩）もニューヨークの建物の建築材料として非常に一般的で、この単語が出てきたらまず間違いなくニューヨーク小説。

⓬ a holy wreath: 聖なる花輪。この一言でクリスマス・シーズンと決まる。

⓭ senses: 五感

⓮ register(ed): 〜を記録する、受けとめる

⓯ painful intensity: 痛々しい強烈さ

⓰ dilated:（クスリ切れのせいで）瞳孔が開いている

⓱ darting his pale blue eyes sideways: 薄青い目をすばやく横に向けて

⓲ in quick appraisal: すばやく値踏みして

⓳ the ventilator windows: 通風窓。一昔前まで車の前方にあった小さな三角窓。

feet. No one in sight. He snapped his fingers and ❶went through a pantomime of remembering something, and ❷wheeled around. No one.

A bad ❸*setup,* he decided. ❹*The street being empty like this, I* ❺*stand out conspicuous.* ❻*Gotta make it fast.*

He ❼reached for the ventilator window. A door opened behind him. Danny ❽whipped out a rag and began polishing the car windows. He could feel the man standing behind him.

"❾What're yuh doin'?"

Danny turned as if surprised. "Just thought your car windows needed polishing, mister."

The man had a frog face and ❿a Deep South accent. He was wearing a camel's-hair overcoat.

"My caah don't need polishin' or ⓫nothing stole out of it neither."

Danny slid sideways as the man ⓬grabbed for him. "⓭I wasn't

❶ went through <go through: いくつか過程のあるしぐさや儀式を行なうことを言う。*The director made the actor go through the scene again.*（監督は俳優にそのシーンをもう一度練習させた。『コンパスローズ英和辞典』）
❷ wheeled around: ぐるっと回った
❸ (a) *setup*: a situation
❹ *The street being empty like this:* Because the street is empty like this
❺ *stand out conspicuous*: ひどく目立つ
❻ *Gotta make it fast*: さっさとやらないと。gotta: I've got to=I have to
❼ reached for ...: ～に手を伸ばした
❽ whipped out a rag: ぼろ切れをさっと取り出した
❾ What're yuh doin'?: What are you doing?
❿ a Deep South accent: 深南部なまり。アメリカ南部のなまりは母音を延ばす

らして、ふと何かを思い出したようなパントマイムを演じ、ぐるっと体を回した。誰もいない。

まずいな、と彼は思った。**街がこんなに空っぽじゃ目立っちまう。さっさと片付けよう。**

三角窓に手を伸ばす。うしろで、どこかの家のドアが開いた。ダニーはボロ切れを取り出して車のウィンドウを拭きはじめた。背後に男が立っているのが感じでわかった。

「何してんだ？」

ダニーは驚いたような顔をしてふり向いた。「いやちょっと、おたくの車、ウィンドウ磨いた方がいいんじゃないかなって思いまして」

男はカエルみたいな顔をしていて、深南部（ディープ・サウス）の訛（なまり）だった。ラクダのコートを着ている。

「磨く必要なんかあるもんか。泥棒にあう必要もな」

つかみかかってくる男をよけてダニーはすっと横に退（の）いた。「いや泥棒だ

(drawl という）のが特徴。l. 14 の “My caah” はその典型。

⓫ nothing stole out of it neither: nothing needs to be stolen out of it either

⓬ grabbed for him: 彼をつかまえようとがばっと手を出した

⓭ I wasn’t lookin’ to ...: I wasn’t planning/going to ...

lookin' to steal nothing, mister. I'm from the South too. Florida—"

"❶Goddamned sneakin' thief!"

Danny walked away fast and turned a corner.

❷*Better get out of* ❸*the neighborhood. That* ❹*hick is likely to call* ❺*the law.*

❻ He walked fifteen blocks. Sweat ran down his body. There was an ache in his lungs. ❼His lips drew back off his yellow teeth ❽in a snarl of desperation.

I gotta ❾*score* ❿*somehow.* ⓫*If I had some decent clothes . . .*

Danny saw a suitcase standing in a doorway. Good leather. He stopped and pretended to look for a cigarette.

Funny, he thought. *No one around. Inside maybe, phoning for a cab.*

The corner was only a few houses away. Danny took a deep breath and picked up the suitcase. ⓬He made the corner. ⓭Another block, another corner. The case was heavy.

❶ Goddamned sneakin' thief: 直訳（?）は「くそいまいましいコソコソはたらく泥棒」。
❷ *Better*: I had better
❸ *the neighborhood*: このあたり
❹ (a) *hick*: 田舎者
❺ *the law*: 警察
❻ He walked fifteen blocks: ニューヨークの街なかの距離を示すには、マイルよりもブロック（四つ角から四つ角まででーブロック）で言う方が多い。
❼ His lips drew back: 唇が引っ込んだ
❽ in a snarl of desperation: 直訳は「絶望によって歯が剥き出されて」。snarlは犬が歯を剥いてうなることなどを言う。
❾ *score*:（スラング）麻薬を手に入れる

なんてそんな、旦那。あたしも南部の出なんですよ。フロリダのね――」

「この汚ねえコソ泥が！」

ダニーはそそくさと立ち去り、角を曲がった。

さっさとこのあたりから離れた方がいい。あの田舎者、下手すりゃ警察呼ぶぜ。

15ブロック歩きつづけた。汗が体じゅうに流れる。肺がひりひり痛んだ。唇が絶望に歪(ゆが)んで、黄色い歯が剝き出しになった。

何とか薬、手に入れなくちゃ。もうちょっとマシな服着てたらなあ……。

ある建物の戸口に、スーツケースが置いてあるのが見えた。上等の革だ。ダニーは立ちどまって、タバコを探すふりをした。

変だな、と彼は思った。**誰もいない。中にいるのかな、電話でタクシーでも呼んでるのか。**

四つ角までは二、三軒だ。ダニーはぐっと深呼吸して、スーツケースを手に取った。四つ角にたどり着き、もう一ブロック歩いて、次の四つ角に着いた。スーツケースは重かった。

⑩ *somehow*: どうにかして。手に入れる手立てが目下ないことを示唆。
⑪ *If I had some decent clothes*: I wish I had some decent clothes. decent: まともな
⑫ He made the corner: 角にたどり着いた
⑬ Another block, another corner: He walked another block, and made another corner

❶*I got a score here all right,* he thought. *Maybe enough for a* ❷*sixteenth and a room.* Danny ❸shivered and twitched, feeling a warm room and heroin ❹emptying into his vein. *Let's have a quick look.*

He stepped into ❺Morningside Park. No one around.

❻*Jesus, I never see the town this empty.*

He opened the suitcase. Two long packages in brown wrapping paper. He took one out. It felt like meat. He ❼tore the package open at one ❽end, revealing a woman's naked foot. The ❾toenails were painted with purple-red ❿polish. He dropped the leg ⓫with a sneer of disgust.

⓬"Holy Jesus!" he exclaimed. "⓭The routines people put down these days. Legs! Well I got a case anyway." He ⓮dumped the other leg out. No ⓯bloodstains. He ⓰snapped the case shut and walked away.

"Legs!" he muttered.

＊

❶ *I got a score here all right*: これでクスリが手に入った。p. 152, l. 9 の *I gotta score somehow* を受けている。all right: たしかに、間違いなく
❷ *a sixteenth*: 16 分の 1 グラム。まあ一回ハイになれる量らしい。
❸ shivered and twitched: 震え、ひきつった
❹ emptying into his vein: 血管に流れ込んで
❺ Morningside Park: マンハッタン北部にある公園。かつては犯罪が多発する物騒な場所として有名だった。
❻ *Jesus*: 驚いた
❼ tore <tear: 〜を裂く、破る
❽ end: 端、先
❾ toenail(s): 足の爪
❿ polish: マニキュア、ペディキュア

こりゃ絶対カネになるぜ、と彼は思った。**うまく行きゃ薬と、宿代も出るかな。**体が震えて、引きつる。暖かい部屋とヘロインが、血管にすーっと流れ込んでくる気がする。**ちょっと見てみようじゃないか。**

モーニングサイド・パークに入っていった。あたりには誰もいない。

参ったぜ、この街がこんなに空っぽだなんて初めてだ。

スーツケースを開けた。細長い包みが二つ、茶色の包み紙にくるんである。ひとつ出してみた。肉か何かみたいだ。包み紙の端を破いてみると、女のむき出しの片脚が出てきた。指の爪にパープルレッドのペディキュアが塗ってある。なんだよこれ、とげっそりして脚をその場に捨てた。

「ふざけやがって！」とダニーは声を上げた。「近ごろの奴らときたら！　脚なんか入れやがって！　ま、とにかくスーツケースはあるからな」。もう一方の脚も放(ほお)った。スーツケースに血のしみは全然ない。ぱちんと閉めて、立ち去った。

「脚かよ！」となおもぶつぶつ言った。

*

⓫ with a sneer of disgust: 嫌悪の念もあらわに。sneer は「冷笑」と訳されることが多いが、侮蔑、嫌悪の念に顔を歪めるのであれば「笑」でなくても構わない。
⓬ Holy Jesus!: なんてこった！
⓭ The routines people put down these days: 近ごろの人間がやらかすロクでもないこと。routines はここでは「手口」程度、また put down は文脈から見て「やってのける」といった意。
⓮ dumped the other leg out: もう一方の脚も投げ捨てた
⓯ bloodstain(s): 血痕
⓰ snapped the case shut: スーツケースをパチンと閉めた

He found the Buyer sitting at a table in Jarrow's Cafeteria.

"❶Thought you might be taking the day off," Danny said, putting the case down.

The Buyer shook his head sadly. "I got nobody. So what's Christmas to me?" His eyes traveled over the case, ❷poking, testing, looking for ❸flaws. "What was in it?"

"Nothing."

"What's the matter? ❹I don't pay enough?"

"I tell you ❺there wasn't nothing in it."

"Okay. So somebody travels with an empty suitcase. Okay." He held up three fingers.

"❻For Christ's sake, Gimpy, give me ❼a nickel."

"You got somebody else. Why don't he give you a nickel?"

"It's like I say, the case was empty."

Gimpy kicked at the case ❽disparagingly. ❾"It's all nicked up and kinda dirty-looking." He ❿sniffed suspiciously. "⓫How come it ⓬stink like that? Mexican leather?"

❶ Thought you might be taking the day off: 今日は休みをとっているかと思った。take a day off: 一日休みをとる
❷ poking <poke: つっつく
❸ flaw(s): 欠陥、疵
❹ I don't pay enough?: 俺の払いじゃ足りないのか？
❺ there wasn't nothing in it: there was nothing in it の標準的でない言い方。
❻ For Christ's sake: いい加減にしてくれよ、冗談じゃないぜ
❼ a nickel: 標準的な英語では「5 セント貨」の意だが、ここではスラングで「5 ドル」。
❽ disparagingly: 蔑むように
❾ It's all nicked up and kinda dirty-looking: そこらじゅう細かい傷だらけで、なんとなく汚く見える。nicked は刻み目、切れ目のような細い傷を言う。

　ジャローズ・カフェテリアのテーブルに、バイヤーが座っていた。
「今日は休んでるかと思ったぜ」とダニーはスーツケースを下ろしながら言った。
　バイヤーは悲しげに首を横に振った。「俺には誰もいねえ。クリスマスがなんだってんだ？」。目がスーツケースを眺めまわし、あちこち押したりつついたりして、あらを探している。「何が入ってたんだ？」
「なんにも」
「どうしたいったい？　俺の払いじゃ不足だってのか？」
「言ってるじゃねえか、なんにも入ってなかったって」
「ああそうかい。どっかの誰かが、空っぽのスーツケースで旅行してたってわけか。そうかいそうかい」。バイヤーは指を３本立てた。
「勘弁してくれよギンピー、５ドルくれよ」
「ほかの奴とも取り引きしてんだろ。そいつに５ドルもらったらどうだ」
「言っただろ、空っぽだったんだよ、初めっから」
　ギンピーは蔑むようにスーツケースを蹴った。「傷だらけだし、なんか薄汚ねえな」。疑わしそうにくんくん鼻を動かす。「なんだよこの臭(にお)い？　メキシコ製の革か？」

kinda: kind of
❿ sniffed suspiciously: 疑わしそうにクンクン嗅いだ
⓫ How come ...?: なんで〜なんだ？
⓬ stink: 臭(くさ)い、臭(にお)う（正しくは stinks）。

[1]"So am I in the leather business?"

Gimpy [2]shrugged. "[3]Could be." He pulled out [4]a roll of bills and [5]peeled off three ones, dropping them on the table behind [6]the napkin dispenser. "[7]You want?"

"Okay." Danny picked up the money. "[8]You see George the Greek?" he asked.

"[9]Where you been? He [10]got busted two days ago."

"Oh . . . That's bad."

Danny walked out. *Now where can I score?* he thought. George the Greek had [11]lasted so long, Danny thought of him as permanent. *It was good [12]H too, and no [13]short counts.*

Danny went up to [14]103rd and Broadway. Nobody in Jarrow's. Nobody in [15]the Automat.

"Yeah," he [16]snarled. "All the [17]pushers [18]off on the nod

[1] So am I in the leather business?: じゃあ俺は革商売ってわけか？　臭いぞ、メキシコ革か、という皮肉に皮肉で返しているが、まああまりシャープではない。
[2] shrug(ged): 肩をすくめる。日本にはまだ定着していないボディランゲージだが、ここでは「まあどっちでもいいんだけどさ」「俺は知らんけど」といった感じ。
[3] Could be: ありうるぜ
[4] a roll of bills: 札の束
[5] peeled off three ones: 一ドル札を三枚剝がした
[6] the napkin dispenser: 紙ナプキン入れ。金属製の、安食堂のテーブルの定番的アイテム。
[7] You want?: Do you want this?
[8] You see George the Greek?: Did you see ...?　Georgeの元の名はおそらく、ギリシャではきわめて一般的な名である「ゲオルギオス」だろう。
[9] Where you been?: Where have you been?
[10] got busted: 捕まった
[11] last(ed): 続く

「俺が革商売やってると思うか？」

ギンピーは肩をすくめた。「かもな」。札の束を引っぱり出して、1ドル札を3枚はがし、テーブルの上、紙ナプキン入れの陰に放り投げた。「どうする？」

「わかったよ」。ダニーは金を取った。「ギリシャ人ジョージ（ジョージ・ザ・グリーク）見かけたかい？」と彼は訊ねた。

「お前どこにいたんだ？　ジョージなら2日前に捕まったぜ」

「そうか……そりゃいけねえな」

ダニーは店を出た。**さて、どこで薬を手に入れよう？**　ジョージ・ザ・グリークはずいぶん長続きしていたから、なんとなく、いつまでもいなくならないような気になっていたのだ。**いいH（ヘロイン）だったし、ごまかしもなかった。**

ブロードウェイ103丁目に行った。ジャローズには誰もいない。無人カフェ（オートマット）にもいない。

「そうだよな」とダニーは吐き捨てるように思った。「売人のやつらみんな、

⓬ *H*: heroin

⓭ *short count(s)*: ドラッグの量がごまかしてあって足りないこと。*I'm always getting a short count when he's serving.*（あいつに頼むといつも量をごまかされる。*The Urban Dictionary*）

⓮ 103rd and Broadway: マンハッタンで場所を伝えるには、このように東西にのびた street（この場合は 103rd Street）と、南北にのびた、おおむねより広い avenue（この場合は Broadway）を言って四つ角を特定するのが一般的。

⓯ the Automat: 20世紀前半に栄えた、自動販売機を並べた無人のファストフード・レストラン。人間のいるファストフード・レストランの隆盛によって淘汰された。

⓰ snarl(ed): 歯を剝く。p. 152, l. 8 の "in a snarl of desperation" と同じ。

⓱ pusher(s): 売人

⓲ off on the nod: どこかへ行ってしまって（off）、朦朧としている（on the nod）

someplace. ❶What they care about anybody else? ❷So long as they ❸get it in the vein. What they care about a sick junky?"

He wiped his nose with one finger, looking around ❹furtively.

❺*No use hitting those jigs in Harlem.* ❻*Like as not* ❼*get beat for my money or they* ❽*slip me rat poison. Might find Pantopon Rose at* ❾*Eighth and 23rd.*

There was no one he knew in the 23rd Street Thompson's.

Jesus, he thought. *Where is everybody?*

He ❿clutched his coat collar together with one hand, looking up and down the street. *There's Joey from Brooklyn.* ⓫*I'd know that hat anywhere.*

"Joey. Hey, Joey!"

Joey was walking away, with his back to Danny. He turned around. His face was ⓬sunken, skull-like. The gray eyes ⓭glittered under a greasy gray felt hat. Joey was ⓮sniffing at regular intervals and his eyes were watering.

❶ What they care about anybody else?: What do they care about anybody else?　むろん本気の自問ではなく、どうせ奴らは care しないんだ、ということ。
❷ So long as ...: 〜しさえすれば
❸ get it in the vein: 血管に（ドラッグを）入れる
❹ furtively: こっそりと
❺ *No use hitting those jigs in Harlem*: ハーレムの黒人たちに頼んだって仕方ない。hit(ting): 〜に頼む／jig(s):（侮蔑的）黒人
❻ *Like as not* <likely as not: おそらく
❼ *get beat*: ごまかされる、ぼられる
❽ *slip me rat poison*: ネコイラズをつかませる
❾ *Eighth and 23rd*: p. 158, l. 12 では street, avenue の順だったが、ここで

どっかでいい気分になってやがるんだ。他人のことなんかどうだっていいと思ってんだ。てめえの血管に入れられさえすりゃいいんだ。病気のジャンキーのことなんか知りやしねえ」

一本の指で鼻を拭い、あたりをこっそり見回した。

ハーレムで黒人の奴ら相手にしたって仕方ねえ。ぼられるか、ネコイラズつかまされるのがオチだ。8番街の23丁目に行ったらパントポン・ローズがいるかな。

23丁目のトンプソンズにも、知り合いは一人もいなかった。

やれやれ、と彼は思った。**みんなどこにいるんだ？**

コートの襟を片手で引き寄せて、通りをきょろきょろ見渡す。**ありゃあブルックリンのジョーイだ。あの帽子、どこで見たってわかるさ。**

「ジョーイ。よう、ジョーイ！」

ジョーイはダニーに背を向けて立ち去ろうとしているところだった。呼ばれてこっちを向いた。顔がくぼんで、頭蓋骨みたいだった。灰色の目が、垢じみた灰色のフェルト帽の下でぎらぎら光っている。ジョーイはくり返し洟(はな)をすすり、目もうるんでいた。

は avenue, street の順になっている。
❿ clutch(ed): ～を摑む
⓫ *I'd know that hat anywhere*: あの帽子はどこで見てもわかる
⓬ sunken, skull-like: くぼんで、頭蓋骨のようで
⓭ glitter(ed): ギラギラ光る
⓮ sniff(ing): 鼻をすする

No use asking him, Danny thought. ❶They looked at each other with the hatred of disappointment.

"Guess you heard about George the Greek," Danny said.

"Yeah. I heard. ❷You been up to 103rd?"

"Yeah. Just came from there. Nobody around."

"Nobody around anyplace," Joey said. "I ❸can't even score for goofballs."

"Well, Merry Christmas, Joey. ❹See you."

"Yeah. See you."

Danny was walking fast. He had remembered ❺a croaker on 18th Street. Of course the croaker had told him not to come back. Still, it was ❻worth trying.

A brownstone house with a card in the window: *P. H. Zunniga,* ❼*M.D.* Danny rang the bell. He heard slow steps. The door opened, and the doctor looked at Danny with ❽bloodshot brown eyes. He

❶ They looked at each other with the hatred of disappointment: 失望が生む憎しみの念とともにたがいを見た。*No use asking him* と考えているのはダニーだけではないだろう。二人はたがいの鏡像である。
❷ You been up to 103rd?: Have you been up to 103rd? up がついているのは 103 丁目がそこより北だから。
❸ can't even score for goofballs: goofball さえ手に入らない。goofball(s): アンフェタミンなどの覚醒剤の錠剤。ドラッグとしては明らかに安物。
❹ See you: じゃあな
❺ a croaker: 医者
❻ worth trying: 試してみる価値はある
❼ *M. D.*: Medicinae Doctor（ラテン語、Doctor of Medicine の意）
❽ bloodshot: 充血した

こいつに頼んでも無駄だな、とダニーは思った。失望が生む憎しみをこめた目で二人はたがいを見た。
「ジョージ・ザ・グリークのことは聞いたろうな」とダニーは言った。
「ああ。聞いた。103丁目に行ったか？」
「ああ。いま行ってきたところだ。誰もいなかった」
「誰もどこにもいないよ」とジョーイは言った。「アンフェタミンも買えやしねえ」
「ま、メリー・クリスマス、ジョーイ。じゃあな」
「ああ。じゃあな」

急ぎ足で歩く。18丁目にいる医者のことを思い出したのだ。もちろんその医者には、二度と来るなと言われている。でもまあ、試してみて損はない。
ブラウンストーン造りの家で、窓に名刺が貼ってある。医学博士P・H・ズニガ。ダニーは呼び鈴を押した。のろのろした足音が聞こえた。ドアが開いて、医者が充血した茶色い目でダニーを見た。少し足がふらついていて、ぼってりした体をドアの側柱に寄りかからせた。ラテン系のつるつるした顔

was ❶weaving slightly and supported his ❷plump body against the ❸doorjamb. His face was smooth, Latin, the little red mouth ❹slack. He said nothing. He just ❺leaned there, looking at Danny.

❻*Goddamned alcoholic,* Danny thought. He smiled.

"Merry Christmas, Doctor."

The doctor did not reply.

"You remember me, Doctor." Danny tried to ❼edge past the doctor, into the house. "I'm sorry to trouble you on Christmas Day, but ❽I've suffered another attack."

"Attack?"

"Yes. ❾Facial neuralgia." Danny twisted one side of his face into a horrible ❿grimace. The doctor ⓫recoiled slightly, and Danny pushed into the dark ⓬hallway.

"Better shut the door or you'll be catching cold," he said ⓭jovially, ⓮shoving the door shut.

The doctor looked at him, his eyes ⓯focusing visibly. "I can't

❶ weaving <weave: ジグザグに歩く（元来は「編む」の意）
❷ plump: ぽっちゃりした
❸ doorjamb:（戸口の）側柱
❹ slack: ゆるい、締まっていない
❺ lean(ed): 寄りかかる、もたれる
❻ *Goddamned*: くそいまいましい
❼ edge: 横向きに進む
❽ I've suffered another attack: また発作を起こしたんです。suffer(ed):（不快なことを）被る
❾ Facial neuralgia: 顔面神経痛
❿ (a) grimace: ゆがんだ顔
⓫ recoil(ed): あとずさりする、ひるむ

で、小さな赤い口はだらんとして締まりがない。医者は何も言わない。ただ寄りかかって、ダニーを見ている。

アル中野郎が、とダニーは思った。にっこり笑顔を作った。

「メリー・クリスマス、先生」

医者は何も言わなかった。

「俺のこと覚えてらっしゃるでしょう、先生」。ダニーは医者の横をすり抜けて家の中へ入ろうとした。「クリスマスの日にお邪魔してすいません、実はまた発作が起きちまいまして」

「発作？」

「はい。顔面神経痛が」。ダニーは顔の片側を思いきり歪めてみせた。医者がわずかにうしろに下がったすきに、暗い玄関広間に押し入った。

「ドア閉めた方がいいですよ、風邪ひきますよ」とダニーは陽気に言って、ドアをすっと押して閉めた。

医者はダニーを見た。目の焦点が見るみる合ってきた。「君には処方は出

⓬ (the) hallway: 玄関
⓭ jovially: 陽気に
⓮ shoving <shove: 〜を押す。push より乱暴な感じ。
⓯ focusing visibly: 目に見えて焦点が合ってきている

give you ❶a prescription," he said.

"But Doctor, this is ❷a legitimate condition. ❸An emergency, you understand."

"No prescription. Impossible. It's against the law."

"❹You took an oath, Doctor. I'm ❺in agony." ❻Danny's voice shot up to a hysterical grating whine.

The doctor ❼winced and ❽passed a hand over his forehead.

"Let me think. I can give you ❾one quarter-grain tablet. That's all I have in the house."

"But, Doctor—a quarter ❿G . . ."

The doctor stopped him. "If your condition is legitimate, you will not need more. If it isn't, ⓫I don't want anything to do with you. ⓬Wait right here."

The doctor weaved down the hall, leaving ⓭a wake of alcoholic breath. He came back and dropped a tablet into Danny's hand. Danny wrapped the tablet in a piece of paper and ⓮tucked it away.

❶ a prescription: 処方箋
❷ a legitimate condition: 正当な、本物の病状
❸ An emergency: 緊急事態
❹ You took an oath, Doctor: 先生、あなたは誓ったでしょう。いわゆるヒポクラテスの誓いのこと。何項目もあるが、特に、患者を利すると思える治療をあたう限り行なう、という趣旨の項をダニーは念頭に置いている。
❺ in agony: 激しい苦痛を覚えている
❻ Danny's voice shot up to a hysterical grating whine: ダニーの声が一気に高くなって(shot up)、ヒステリックな、耳障りな(grating)情けない声(whine)になった。whine は p. 134, l. 3 の whining と同じ。
❼ wince(d): 気まずさ、不快さゆえに思わず顔を歪めること。
❽ passed a hand over his forehead: 額に手を滑らせた。若干の狼狽が感じら

せん」と医者は言った。

「でも先生、こいつは本物の症状なんですよ。緊急なんですよ、わかるでしょう」

「処方は出せん。絶対駄目だ。法律違反だ」

「先生、先生だって医師としての誓いはなさったでしょう。俺は激痛に苦しんでるんですよ」。ダニーの声がヒステリックな、きしむような情けない響きに変わった。

医者はうろたえて、片手を額に滑らせた。

「そうだな。四分の一グレーンの錠剤なら出してもいいかな。ここにはそれしかない」

「でも先生――四分の一Gじゃ……」

医者がその言葉をさえぎった。「症状が本物なんだったらそれ以上は要らんはずだ。本物じゃないんだったら、君とかかわるのはごめんだ。ここで待ってなさい」

医者は千鳥足で廊下を歩いていった。酒くさい息が残った。戻ってきて、錠剤を一粒、ダニーの手のひらに落とした。ダニーはそれを紙に包んでしまい込んだ。

れる。

❾ one quarter-grain tablet: 4分の1グレーンの錠剤をひとつ。1グレーンは約65mg。

❿ G: grain

⓫ I don't want anything to do with you: 君とは関係を持ちたくない

⓬ Wait right here: ここで待っていなさい。right は軽い強調。

⓭ a wake:（航跡などの）跡

⓮ tucked it away: しまい込んだ

"There is no ❶charge." The doctor put his hand on the doorknob. "And now, my dear . . ."

"But, Doctor—can't you ❷inject the medication?"

"No. You will ❸obtain longer relief in using orally. ❹Please not to return." The doctor opened the door.

Well, ❺this will take the edge off, and I still have money to ❻put down on a room, Danny thought.

He knew a drugstore that sold needles without question. He bought ❼a 26-gauge insulin needle and ❽an eyedropper, which he selected carefully, ❾rejecting models with a curved dropper or a thick end. Finally he bought ❿a baby pacifier, to use instead of ⓫the bulb. He stopped in the Automat and stole a teaspoon.

Danny put down two dollars on a six-dollar-a-week room in the West Forties, where he knew the landlord. He ⓬bolted the door and put his spoon, needle and dropper on a table by the bed. He dropped the tablet in the spoon and covered it with ⓭a dropperful

❶ charge: 料金
❷ inject the medication: 薬剤を注射する
❸ obtain longer relief in using orally: 内服で（orally）用いることで、より長い苦痛の軽減（relief）を得る（obtain）
❹ Please not to return: Please don't / do not return よりよそよそしい感じ。
❺ *this will take the edge off*: これで edge が減るだろう。edge はこの場合、クスリ切れの辛さのこと。
❻ *put down on a room*: 部屋の手付金を払う
❼ a 26-gauge insulin needle: gauge は注射針の外径の単位。26-gauge は標準的な太さのようである。
❽ an eyedropper: 点眼器、スポイト
❾ rejecting models with a curved dropper or a thick end: 点眼部がカーブ

「料金は要らん」。医者は片手をドアノブにかけた。「さあ、これで……」

「でも先生――注射はしてもらえないんですか？」

「駄目だ。経口薬の方が長く効くはずだ。もう来ないでくれたまえ」。医者はドアを開けた。

ま、これで少しは楽になるし、宿代の手付金も残る、とダニーは思った。

何も聞かずに針を売ってくれる薬局がある。ダニーはそこへ行った。26ゲージのインシュリン針と、スポイトを慎重に選んで――曲がってるのや先が太くなってるのは駄目だ――買った。最後に、スポイトのゴムの代わりに使うおしゃぶりを買った。無人カフェに寄って、ティースプーンを失敬した。

西40丁目台にある、なじみの大家がやっている週6ドルの部屋の手付を2ドル払った。ドアの差し錠を締めて、スプーン、針、スポイトをベッドのそばのテーブルに置いた。錠剤をスプーンに落とし、スポイト一杯ぶんの水

していたり、端が太かったりする製品を退けて

⑩ a baby pacifier: おしゃぶり

⑪ the bulb: スポイトのゴム

⑫ bolted the door: ドアの差し錠を締めた

⑬ a dropperful of water: 点眼器一杯分の水

of water. He held a match under the spoon until the tablet ❶dissolved. He tore a strip of paper, wet it and wrapped it around the end of the dropper, ❷fitting the needle over the wet paper ❸to make an airtight connection. He dropped a piece of ❹lint from his pocket into the spoon and ❺sucked the liquid into the dropper through the needle, holding the needle in the lint ❻to take up the last drop.

Danny's hands ❼trembled with excitement and his breath was quick. ❽With a shot in front of him, ❾his defenses gave way, and ❿junk sickness flooded his body. His legs began to ⓫twitch and ache. ⓬A cramp ⓭stirred in his stomach. Tears ran down his face from his ⓮smarting, burning eyes. He wrapped a handkerchief around his right arm, holding the end in his teeth. He ⓯tucked the handkerchief in, and began rubbing his arm to ⓰bring out a vein.

⓱*Guess I can hit that one*, he thought, running one finger along a vein. He picked up the dropper in his left hand.

❶ dissolve(d): 溶ける
❷ fitting the needle over the wet paper: 濡れた紙に針をきっちり差し入れて
❸ to make an airtight connection: 直訳は「空気漏れのないつなぎを作るために」。
❹ lint: 糸くず
❺ suck(ed): ～を吸い込む
❻ to take up the last drop: 最後の一滴を吸わせるために
❼ tremble(d): 震える
❽ With a shot in front of him: クスリの注射（shot）を目前に控えて
❾ his defenses gave way: 彼の防御が崩れた
❿ junk sickness flooded his body: クスリ切れの辛さが体じゅうにあふれた
⓫ twitch and ache: ひきつり、痛む

を上にかけた。スプーンの下にマッチをかざして、錠剤が溶けるまで火であぶる。紙切れを破いて濡らし、スポイトの端をそれで包んで、そこに針をきっちり差し込んで空気が漏れないようにする。ポケットから糸くずの塊を出してスプーンに落とし、針を通して液体をスポイトに吸い込んで、おしまいに針を糸くずで押さえて最後の一滴を吸わせた。

ダニーの手が興奮に震え、息も速まった。いよいよ打てるかと思うと、ガードも解けてきて、薬の切れた苦しみが体じゅうにどっとあふれてきた。両脚が引きつり、痛みはじめた。胃も痙攣してきた。ひりひり痛む目から涙があふれ、顔を流れ落ちた。ハンカチの端を歯でくわえて右腕に巻きつけた。ハンカチをたくし込んで、血管を浮き立たせようと腕をこすった。

こいつで行けそうだな、と彼は思って、指を一本、血管にそって滑らせた。左手でスポイトを取り上げた。

⓬ A cramp: 痙攣
⓭ stir(red): うごめく
⓮ smarting: ひりひり痛む
⓯ tucked the handkerchief in: ハンカチをたくし込んだ
⓰ bring out a vein: 血管を浮かび上がらせる
⓱ *Guess I can hit that one*:（浮かび上がった血管を見ながら）こいつに打てそうだな

Danny heard ❶a groan from the next room. He ❷frowned with annoyance. Another groan. He could not help listening. He ❸walked across the room, the dropper in his hand, and ❹inclined his ear to the wall. The groans were coming ❺at regular intervals, a horrible ❻inhuman sound pushed out from the stomach.

Danny listened for a full minute. He returned to the bed and sat down. *Why don't someone call a doctor?* he thought ❼indignantly. ❽*It's a bringdown.* He straightened his arm and ❾poised the needle. He ❿tilted his head, listening again.

⓫*Oh, for Christ's sake!* He ⓬tore off the handkerchief and placed the dropper in a water glass, which he hid behind ⓭the wastebasket. He ⓮stepped into the hall and knocked on the door of the next room. There was no answer. The groans continued. Danny ⓯tried the door. It was open.

⓰The shade was up and the room was full of light. He had ⓱expected an old person somehow, but the man on the bed was

❶ a groan: うめき声
❷ frowned with annoyance: 苛立って眉をひそめた
❸ walked across the room: 部屋の向こう側に歩いていった。across という言葉を訳すとき、「横切って」は避けた方がいいことが多い。
❹ incline(d): 〜を傾ける
❺ at regular intervals: 一定の間隔で
❻ inhuman: 人間とは思えない
❼ indignantly: 憤って
❽ *It's a bringdown*: 白けるぜ、興ざめだ
❾ poise(d): 〜を構える
❿ tilt(ed): 〜を傾ける
⓫ *Oh, for Christ's sake!*: ああ、いいかげんにしてくれ！

と、隣の部屋からうめき声が聞こえた。なんだよこんな時に、とダニーは顔をしかめた。またうめき声。聞くまいと思っても聞こえてしまう。スポイトを持ったまま部屋の向こう側まで行って、耳を壁に押しつけた。うめき声は一定の間隔で聞こえてきた。下腹から絞り出されてくる、ぞっとする、人間とは思えない声。

ダニーはまる一分耳を澄ましていた。ベッドに戻って、腰を下ろした。**どうして誰か医者を呼んでやらないんだ？**　と彼は憤慨した。**嫌んなるぜまったく。**腕をまっすぐ伸ばして、針を構えた。首を傾けて、また耳を澄ました。

くそ、ふざけやがって！　ハンカチを剝ぎ取って、スポイトをコップに入れ、屑かごのうしろに隠した。廊下に出て、隣の部屋のドアをノックした。返事はない。うめき声はまだ続いている。ドアを押してみた。鍵はかかっていなかった。

ブラインドは上がっていて、部屋じゅうに陽がさしていた。なんとなく老人を予想していたが、ベッドの上の男はひどく若く、18か、せいぜい20（はたち）だ。

⓬ tore off the handkerchief: ハンカチを乱暴に取った
⓭ the wastebasket: くずかご
⓮ stepped into the hall: 廊下に歩み出た
⓯ tried the door: （鍵がかかっているかどうかわからない）ドアを開けようとしてみた
⓰ The shade: ブラインド
⓱ expected an old person somehow: なぜか年寄りを予想していた。「期待していた」ではない。

very young, eighteen or twenty, fully clothed and ❶doubled up, ❷with his hands clasped across his stomach.

"What's wrong, kid?" Danny asked.

The boy looked at him, his eyes ❸blank with pain. Finally he got out one word: "❹Kidneys."

"❺Kidney stones?" Danny smiled. "❻I don't mean it's funny, kid. ❼It's just . . . I've ❽faked it so many times. Never saw the real thing before. I'll call ❾an ambulance."

The boy ❿bit his lip. "Won't come. Doctors won't come." The boy hid his face in the pillow.

Danny nodded. "⓫They figure ⓬it's just another junky⓭throwing a wingding ⓮for a shot. But your case is ⓯legit. Maybe if I went to the hospital and explained things . . . No, I guess that wouldn't be so good."

"Don't live here," the boy said, ⓰his voice muffled. "They say ⓱I'm not entitled."

❶ doubled up: 体を二つに折り曲げて

❷ with his hands clasped across his stomach: 腹の上で両手をぎゅっと合わせて

❸ blank: うつろな

❹ Kidney(s): 腎臓

❺ Kidney stone(s): 腎臓結石

❻ I don't mean it's funny: いや、笑えるっていうんじゃないぜ

❼ It's just ...: ただ、〜

❽ faked it so many times: 何度もそのふりをした

❾ an ambulance: 救急車

❿ bit <bite: 〜を噛む

⓫ They figure: they think

上着も脱がず横になって、体を半分に折り曲げ、両手で腹を押さえつけている。

「どうした、小僧？」とダニーは訊いた。

若者はダニーを見た。痛みで目がうつろだった。やっとのことで、一言絞り出した。「腎臓」

「腎臓結石か？」ダニーはニヤッと笑って言った。「いや、べつにからかってんじゃないぜ。ただその……俺もその手はずいぶん使ったからさ。本物見るの、初めてなんだ。救急車呼んでやるよ」

若者は唇を噛んだ。「来やしないよ。医者なんか来ないよ」。若者は顔を枕で隠した。

ダニーはうなずいた。「どうせまたジャンキーが薬切らして暴れてるって思われちまうんだな。でもお前の症状は本物だろ。俺が病院へ行って説明したらさ……いや、それもうまかないだろうな」

「ここに住んでないから」と若者はくぐもった声で言った。「権利がないっ

⓬ it's just another ...: どうせまたいつもの〜だ
⓭ throwing a wingding: クスリ切れの発作を起こして
⓮ for a shot: 注射を求めて
⓯ legit: legitimate
⓰ his voice muffled: くぐもった声で
⓱ I'm not entitled:（ここに住んでいないから）俺には権利がない

"Yeah, ❶I know how they are, the ❷bureaucrat bastards. I had a friend once, died of ❸snakebite ❹right in the waiting room. They wouldn't even listen when he tried to explain a snake bit him. He never had enough ❺moxie. That was fifteen years ago, down in ❻Jacksonville. . . ."

Danny ❼trailed off. Suddenly he put out his thin, dirty hand and touched the boy's shoulder.

"❽I—I'm sorry, kid. You wait. ❾I'll fix you up."

He went back to his room and got the dropper, and returned to the boy's room.

"❿Roll up your sleeve, kid." The boy ⓫fumbled his coat sleeve with a weak hand.

"That's okay. I'll get it." Danny ⓬undid the shirt button at the wrist and pushed the shirt and coat up, ⓭baring a thin brown forearm. ⓮Danny hesitated, looking at the dropper. Sweat ran down his nose. The boy was looking up at him. Danny shoved the

❶ I know how they are: どういう奴らかはわかる
❷ bureaucrat bastards: 役人のクズども
❸ a snakebite: ヘビに噛まれた傷
❹ right in the waiting room: rightは、せっかく待合室まで来ていたのに、という感じ。
❺ moxie: 元気、活力
❻ Jacksonville: フロリダ州北東部の市。ウェブを見てみると、たとえば2018年10月にこの市でsnakebiteが急増している、といった記述がある。
❼ trailed off: 先細りになって消えた
❽ I—I'm sorry: 謝っているというより、気の毒がっている。
❾ I'll fix you up: 俺が治してやる
❿ Roll up your sleeve: 袖をまくれ

て言うんだ」

「ああ、わかるよ、病院の奴らってのはそうなんだ、役人根性丸出しでさ。俺の昔の友だちなんか、ヘビに噛まれて、待合室まで行ったのに死んじまったよ。ヘビに噛まれたんですって言っても全然聞いてもらえなくてさ。もともと元気ない奴だったなあ。もう15年になるな、あれはジャクソンヴィルの……」

ダニーの声が尻切れになった。出し抜けに、痩せて汚れた片手をつき出して、若者の肩に触った。

「気――気の毒にな、小僧。待ってな。俺がなんとかしてやる」

自分の部屋に戻って、スポイトを持ち出して、もう一度若者の部屋に行った。

「袖をまくりな、小僧」。若者は弱々しい手つきで上着の袖をもぞもぞ動かした。

「よしよし、無理すんな。俺がやってやる」。シャツの袖のボタンを外してやり、シャツと上着を押し上げた。痩せた茶色い腕が現われた。ダニーはスポイトを見ながら、ためらった。汗が鼻を伝って流れた。若者は彼を見上げ

⓫ fumble(d): ～をいじくる
⓬ undid <undo:（ボタンなどを）外す
⓭ baring a thin brown forearm: 痩せた茶色い前腕をむき出しにして
⓮ Danny hesitated: 自分のクスリ切れは解消できなくなるのだから無理もない。

needle in the boy's forearm and ❶watched the liquid drain into the flesh. He straightened up.

The boy's face began to relax. He ❷sat up and smiled.

"❸Say, ❹that stuff really works," he said. "You a doctor, mister?"

"No, kid."

The boy lay down, stretching. "I feel ❺real sleepy. Didn't sleep ❻all last night." His eyes were closing.

Danny walked across the room and pulled the shade down. He went back to his room and closed the door without locking it. He sat on the bed, looking at the empty dropper. It was getting dark outside. Danny's body ❼ached for junk, but it was a ❽dull ache now, dull and hopeless. ❾Numbly, he took the needle off the dropper and wrapped it in a piece of paper. Then he wrapped the needle and dropper together. He sat there with the package in his hand. ❿*Gotta stash this someplace,* he thought.

❶ watched the liquid drain into the flesh: 液体が体（the flesh）に流れ込む（drain）のを見守った
❷ sat up: 上半身を起こした
❸ Say: ねえ
❹ that stuff really works: いまのやつ、ほんとに効く。stuff はほとんどあらゆる「物」を指しうる。
❺ real sleepy: 口語では really sleepy より普通なくらい。「すごく眠い」ではなく「すごい眠い」という感じ。
❻ all last night: 昨夜ずっと
❼ ached for junk: クスリを欲して疼いた
❽ dull: 鈍い
❾ Numbly: ぼうっとして

ている。ダニーは若者の腕に針を突き刺し、液体が体内に流れていくのを見守った。ダニーは背筋を伸ばした。

若者の顔がリラックスしてきた。体を起こして、笑みを浮かべた。

「いやあ、これ、効くんだねえ」と若者は言った。「あんたお医者さんなの、ミスター？」

「いや違うよ、小僧」

若者は横になって、体を伸ばした。「すごい眠いよ。昨日の夜は全然眠れなかったんだ」。目がもう閉じかけていた。

ダニーは窓辺に行ってブラインドを下ろした。自分の部屋へ戻って、ドアを閉めた。鍵はかけなかった。ベッドに腰かけて、空っぽのスポイトを見た。外は暗くなりかけていた。ダニーの体が薬を求めて疼いたが、いまやそれは鈍い疼きだった。鈍い、望みのない疼き。ぼうっとした頭で、針をスポイトから外して、紙切れでくるんだ。それから針とスポイトを一緒に包んだ。包みを手に持ったまま、そこに座っていた。**こいつをどこかに隠さなくちゃ**、と彼は思った。

⑩ *Gotta stash this someplace:* I have to hide this somewhere

Suddenly a warm flood ❶pulsed through his veins and ❷broke in his head ❸like a thousand golden speedballs.

❹*For Christ's sake,* Danny thought. ❺*I must have scored for the immaculate fix!*

❻The vegetable serenity of junk ❼settled in his tissues. His face went slack and peaceful, and his head fell forward.

Danny the Car Wiper was ❽on the nod.

❶ pulsed through his veins: 脈打って血管を貫いていった
❷ broke in his head: 頭の中で炸裂した
❸ like a thousand golden speedballs: 無数の最高のスピードボールみたいに。speedballs はコカインにヘロイン・モルヒネなどを混ぜたドラッグ。名前からして p. 162, l. 7 の goofballs よりだいぶ高級そうである。
❹ *For Christ's sake*: ここは憤っているのではなく、「こりゃすげえ」という感じ。
❺ *I must have scored for the immaculate fix*: 直訳は「これはきっと immaculate でクスリが手に入ったにちがいない」。fix は「クスリ一回分」だが、immaculate は麻薬用語ではなく、聖母マリアの the Immaculate Conception を踏まえている。厳密には、マリアが原罪を免れた状態で母の子宮に宿ったことを指すが、彼女自身が性行為を経ずにイエスを孕んだこと（いわゆる「処女懐胎」）と混同されることも多い。ここでも実はその方がわかりやすい（性

突然、温かい洪水が血管に脈打ち、頭のなかで、無数の最高のスピードボールみたいに炸裂した。

参ったぜ、とダニーは思った。**こりゃ薬なしで来たらしいぞ！　マリア様みたいだ！**

薬のもたらす、植物のような静けさが体内の組織に染みわたっていった。ダニーの顔が緩んで、安らぎ、頭ががくんと前に落ちた。

車拭きのダニーは、いい気持ちだった。

行為なしで妊娠したマリア＝注射を打たずに「来た」ダニー というアナロジー)。

❻ the vegetable serenity: 植物のような静謐(せいひつ)さ

❼ settled in his tissues: 体内組織に落ち着いていった

❽ on the nod: p. 158, l. 14 に同じだが、文字どおり「うとうと眠っている」というイメージはいっそう強い。

ちなみに

この短篇は 1994 年、Nick Donkin と Melodie McDaniel によってクレイアニメ化されている。製作はフランシス・コッポラ。作者バロウズ自身が朗読した、アニメとしての質も大変高い作品で、原作をほぼ忠実に再現しているが、あいにくダニーがクスリを打とうとする場面をはじめ、クスリ関係のシーンはさすがにいささかぼかした作りになっている。YouTube で見ることができる。

A Village After Dark

Kazuo Ishiguro

日の暮れた村

カズオ・イシグロ

カズオ・イシグロ
(Kazuo Ishiguro, 1954-)

長崎に生まれ育ち、5 歳でイングランドに移住。1982 年 *A Pale View of Hills* を発表して以来、数年に一冊の割合で、高水準の長篇小説を着実に発表しつづけている。記憶、過去の曖昧さが一貫して主要テーマだが、その中で一作一作新しい可能性を切り拓いている。2017 年、ノーベル文学賞受賞。最新作 *Klara and the Sun* は 2021 年 3 月 2 日に世界各国で同時発売された。本作 "A Village After Dark" は *The New Yorker* 誌 2001 年 5 月 21 日号に掲載された。

There was a time when I could travel England ❶for weeks on end and ❷remain at my sharpest—when, ❸if anything, ❹the travelling gave me an edge. But ❺now that I am older I ❻become disoriented more easily. ❼So it was that on arriving at the village just after dark I ❽failed to find my bearings at all. I could hardly believe I was in the same village in which not so long ago I had lived and ❾come to exercise such influence.

There was nothing I ❿recognised, and ⓫I found myself walking forever around ⓬twisting, badly lit streets ⓭hemmed in on both sides by the little stone cottages ⓮characteristic of the area. The streets often became so narrow I could make no progress without my bag or my elbow ⓯scraping one rough wall or another. I ⓰persevered nevertheless, ⓱stumbling around in the darkness ⓲in

❶ for weeks on end: 何週間も続けて
❷ remain at my sharpest: 最高に鋭敏な状態のままでいる
❸ if anything: 何かあるとしても、むしろ逆に
❹ the travelling gave me an edge: give ... an edge は普通「〜を有利にする」の意だが、ここは文字どおり「〜に鋭さを与える」という意味が強い。
❺ now that I am older: 前より年をとったいま
❻ become disoriented:（頭が混乱して）自分がいまどこにいるのか、わからなくなる
❼ So it was that ...: というわけで〜という結果になった
❽ failed to find my bearings at all: 自分がいまどういう位置にいるのか全然わからなかった。bearing(s) は文字どおりには「方位」の意だが、もう少し広く「自分の立場、状況」という意味になることが多い。
❾ (had) come to exercise such influence: それほどの影響力を及ぼすようになった。come to ... は、時を経るなかで何らかの考えや力を持つようになることを言う。
❿ recognise(d): 何かを見て「ああ、あれは何々だ」とわかったり、誰かを見て

かつてはイングランドを何週間も続けて旅しても、頭がこの上なく冴えたままでいられたものだった。むしろ、旅することでいっそう鋭さが増したくらいである。だが、もうそこまで若くないいま、私は前より簡単に混乱してしまう。かくして、日の暮れた直後に村に着いたときも、私には西も東もわからなかった。ここが、さほど遠くない昔に自分が暮らし、大きな勢力をふるうようになった村だとはとうてい信じられなかった。

見覚えのあるものは何ひとつなく、ふと我に返ると、曲がりくねった、照明も粗末な狭い街路をぐるぐる果てしなく歩いているのだった。この地方特有の、小さな石造りのコテージが両側から迫ってくる。街路はしばしばひどく狭くなって、ざらざらの左右の壁どちらかに鞄や肱を擦らないことには一歩も進めぬところも多かった。それでも何とか、暗闇のなかをおぼつかぬ足

「あ、どこそこで見た人だ」とわかったりすることを言う。*I didn't recognise you in your uniform.*（制服を着てるんで見違えてしまったよ。*Longman Dictionary of Contemporary English*）

⓫ I found myself walking ...:「歩いている自分を発見した」というほどの忘我状態を言っているわけではないが、そうするつもりはなかったのに何となくそうしてしまっていた、という含みはこの場合たしかにある。

⓬ twisting, badly lit streets: 曲がりくねった、照明も乏しい街路

⓭ hemmed in on both sides by ...: 両側から〜に囲まれている

⓮ characteristic of ...: 〜特有の

⓯ scraping one rough wall or another: どちらかのごつごつの壁に擦ってしまう

⓰ persevered nevertheless: それでも屈せずに続けた

⓱ stumbling <stumble: よたよた歩く

⓲ in the hope of coming upon the village square: 村の広場に偶然行きつくことを期待して。the village square は昔であれば市 (いち) が立ったり集会が開かれたりする場所。

the hope of coming upon the village square—where I could at least ❶orient myself— ❷or else of encountering one of the villagers. When after a while I had done neither, ❸a weariness came over me, and I decided my best course was just to choose a cottage at random, knock on the door, and hope it would be opened by someone who remembered me.

I stopped by a particularly ❹rickety-looking door, whose upper ❺beam was so low that I could see I would have to ❻crouch right down to enter. A ❼dim light was ❽leaking out around the door's edges, and I could hear voices and laughter. I knocked loudly to ❾insure that the ❿occupants would ⓫hear me over their talk. But just then someone behind me said, 'Hello.'

I turned to find a young woman of around twenty, dressed in ⓬raggedy jeans and a torn jumper, standing in the darkness ⓭a little way away.

'⓮You walked straight past me earlier,' she said, 'even though I

❶ orient myself: 自分の位置を見定める
❷ or else: でなければ
❸ a weariness came over me: 疲労が私を襲った。come over は何か強い感情や体感がにわかに訪れるときに使う。
❹ rickety-looking: ぐらぐらに見える
❺ (a) beam: 梁
❻ crouch right down: しっかりかがみ込む
❼ dim: 薄暗い
❽ leaking out <leak out: 漏れ出る
❾ insure that ...: 確実に〜になるようにする
❿ occupant(s): (部屋などに) いる人
⓫ hear me over their talk: 話し声にも消されずに私のノックの音を聞く。*His*

取りで歩きながら、村の広場にたどりつければと念じていた。広場に出ればとにかく方角はわかるはずだし、広場が駄目でも誰か村人に出会えればありがたい。しばらくして、依然どちらも果たせずにいると、疲れが襲ってきた。ここはひとつ、行き当たりばったりにどこかのコテージを選んで、ドアをノックし、私のことを覚えてくれている人間が開けてくれるのを期待するのが最善の手だと決めた。

とりわけ危なっかしく見える玄関扉の前で、私は立ちどまった。扉上部の梁(はり)がものすごく低く垂れていて、入るには相当背を丸めなければなるまい。扉の四辺から薄ぼんやりした明かりが漏れていて、話したり笑ったりする声が聞こえた。喋っている人たちにもちゃんと聞こえるよう、私は大きな音を立ててノックした。ところがそのとき、背後で誰かが「こんにちは」と言った。

ふり向くと、二十歳(はたち)前後の、ぼろぼろのジーンズに破れたセーターという格好の女性が、少し離れた闇のなかに立っていた。

「さっき声をかけたのに、黙って通りすぎたわね」と彼女は言った。

voice was heard over the noise.（騒音にもかき消されず彼の声が聞こえた。『コンパスローズ英和辞典』）

⓬ raggedy jeans and a torn jumper: ずたずたのジーンズと破れたセーター。a jumper はイギリス英語で「セーター」。日本語の「ジャンパー」は英語では a windbreaker。

⓭ a little way away: 少し離れたところに

⓮ You walked straight past me: 私の横を、立ちどまりもせず歩いていった。straight は直線的ということ以上に、目もくれずに通り過ぎた、という含み。

called to you.'

'Did I really? Well, I'm sorry. ❶I didn't mean to be rude.'

'You're Fletcher, aren't you?'

'Yes,' I said, ❷somewhat flattered.

'Wendy thought it was you when you ❸went by our cottage. We all got very excited. You were ❹one of that lot, weren't you? ❺With David Maggis and all of them.'

'Yes,' I said, 'but Maggis was hardly the most important one. I'm surprised you ❻pick him out like that. There were other, far more important ❼figures.' I ❽reeled off a series of names and was interested to see the girl ❾nodding at each one in recognition. 'But this must have all been ❿before your time,' I said. 'I'm surprised you know about such things.'

'It was before our time, but we're all experts on your lot. We know more about all that than most of the older ones who were here then. Wendy recognised you instantly just from your photos.'

❶ I didn't mean to be rude: 無礼な真似をするつもりはなかった

❷ somewhat flattered: 幾分気をよくして。flatter は「〜にお世辞を言う」の意だが、be/feel flattered だと「褒められて気分がよくなる」という意味。

❸ went by our cottage: 私たちのコテージの前を通り過ぎた

❹ one of that lot: あのグループの一員

❺ with David Maggis and all of them: デイヴィッド・マギスや彼らすべてと一緒に＝デイヴィッド・マギスなんかと一緒に

❻ pick him out like that: そんなふうに彼を選び出す

❼ figure(s): 人物

❽ reeled off a series of names: ひと連なりの名前をすらすら挙げた

❾ nodding at each one in recognition: その一つひとつに対し、いかにも知っているという様子でうなずき。p. 184, l. 8 の recognise の註を参照。

「そうだったんですか？　そりゃどうも失敬。礼を失するつもりはなかったんだが」

「あなた、フレッチャーでしょう？」

「ええ」と私は、いささか気をよくして言った。

「さっきあたしたちのコテージの前を通ったとき、きっとあなただってウェンディが言ったのよ。あたしたちみんなすごく興奮したわ。あなた、あのグループの一人だったんでしょ？　デイヴィッド・マギスなんかと一緒に」

「ええ」と私は言った。「でもマギスは全然、重要人物なんかじゃなかったですよ。君がそうやって奴の名を選び出すとは意外ですね。もっとずっと重要な人間が、ほかに何人もいたのに」。私がいくつか名前を並べてみせると、興味深いことにその娘は、一人ひとりの名前を認識してうなずいていた。「でもみんな君が生まれる前の話でしょう」と私は言った。「驚きだな、そんなことまで知っているとは」

「生まれる前の話だけど、あたしたちみんな、あなたたちのグループのことすごく詳しいのよ。あのころここにいた大方の年上の人たちより、何もかもずっとよく知ってるわ。ウェンディもあなたの写真だけを頼りに、一目であなただと見抜いたのよ」

⑩ before your time: 君が生まれる前

'❶I had no idea you young people had taken such an interest in us. I'm sorry I walked past you earlier. But you see, now that I'm older, I get a little disoriented when I travel.'

I could hear some ❷boisterous talk coming from behind the door. I ❸banged on it again, this time rather ❹impatiently, though I was not so eager to ❺bring the encounter with the girl to a close.

She looked at me for a moment, then said, 'All of you from those days are like that. David Maggis came here a few years ago. In '93, or maybe it was '94. He was like that. ❻A bit vague. ❼It must get to you ❽after a while, travelling all the time.'

'So Maggis was here. How interesting. You know, he wasn't one of the really important figures. ❾You mustn't get carried away with such an idea. ❿Incidentally, perhaps you could tell me who lives in this cottage.' I ⓫thumped the door again.

'The Petersons,' the girl said. '⓬They're an old house. They'll probably remember you.'

❶ I had no idea ...: ～だとは知らなかった
❷ boisterous: 騒々しい
❸ banged on it: どんどんと叩いた
❹ impatiently: せわしなく
❺ bring the encounter with the girl to a close: 直訳は「女の子との出会いを終わりに持っていく」。
❻ A bit vague: ちょっとぼんやりしていて
❼ It must get to you: こたえてくるにちがいない。It はそのあと travelling all the time と具体的に言い換えられている。
❽ after a while: しばらくすると
❾ You mustn't get carried away with such an idea: 直訳は「そんな考えに運び去られてはいけない」。get/be carried away で、何かに夢中になって、

「知らなかったね、君たち若い人が我々にそんなに興味を持ってくれているとは。さっきは黙って行ってしまって申し訳なかった。でもね、私ももう歳なもので、旅をするとどうも混乱してしまうんだよ」

騒々しい話し声が扉のなかから聞こえた。もう一度ドンドンと、今回は相当せっかちに扉を叩いたが、べつに娘との出会いをさっさと終えたいわけではなかった。

娘はしばし私の顔を見てから、言った。「あのころの人たちってみんなそうなのよね。デイヴィッド・マギスも何年か前にここへ来たわ。93年か、ひょっとしたら94年だったかも。あの人もそんなふうだった。ちょっとぼうっとしていて。年中旅をしてると、いずれこたえてくるのね」

「じゃあマギスも来たのか。それはそれは。あいつはね、本当に重要な人物じゃなかったんだ。そんなふうに思い込んじゃいけないよ。ところで、このコテージに誰が住んでるか教えてもらえないかな」。私はもう一度扉を叩いた。

「ピーターソン一家よ」と娘は言った。「年寄りの家族よ。たぶんあなたのこと覚えてるんじゃないかしら」

全体を見失ってしまうことを言う。

⑩ Incidentally: それはそうと

⑪ thump(ed): ドンと叩く

⑫ They're an old house: they are an old family

'The Petersons,' I repeated, but the name ❶meant nothing to me.

'❷Why don't you come to our cottage? Wendy was really excited. So were the rest of us. It's a real chance for us, actually talking to someone from those days.'

'I'd very much like to do that. But first of all I'd better ❸get myself settled in. The Petersons, you say.'

I thumped the door again, this time quite ❹ferociously. At last it opened, throwing warmth and light out into the street. An old man was standing in ❺the doorway. He looked at me carefully, then asked, 'It's not Fletcher, is it?'

'Yes, and I've just got into the village. I've been travelling for several days.'

He thought about this for a moment, then said, '❻Well, you'd better come in.'

❼I found myself in ❽a cramped, untidy room full of rough

❶ meant nothing to me: 私には何も意味しなかった＝何の記憶も浮かんでこなかった
❷ Why don't you come to our cottage?: 私たちのコテージに来ませんか？「なぜ～しないのか」と問うているのではない。
❸ get myself settled in: 腰を落ちつける
❹ ferociously: すさまじく
❺ the doorway: 戸口
❻ Well, you'd better come in: まあ中に入ってもらうか。熱心に招き入れているというよりは、なかば仕方なく入れている感じ。
❼ I found myself in ...: この find oneself は p. 184, l. 8 と同様で、「入ってみるとそこは～だった」というニュアンス。
❽ a cramped, untidy room: 狭苦しく散らかった部屋

「ピーターソン」と私は鸚鵡返しに言ったが、まるで聞き覚えのない名前だった。

「あたしたちのコテージに来たら？　ウェンディはほんとに興奮してたのよ。あたしたちみんな興奮してた。あのころの人と実際に話ができるなんて、すごいチャンスだもの」

「ぜひそうさせていただきたいね。でもまずは、どこかに腰を落着けた方がいいと思うんだ。ここはピーターソン一家の家なんだね」

私はもう一度、今回はすさまじい勢いでノックした。やっとのことで扉が開いて、暖かい空気と光が街路にあふれ出てきた。老人が一人、戸口に立っていた。老人は私をじっくり眺め、それから「フレッチャーじゃないよな？」と訊いた。

「フレッチャーだとも、たったいま村に着いたんだ。何日も旅してきたんだよ」

それを聞いて老人は少しのあいだ考えていたが、やがて「ま、入ってもらうしかないな」と言った。

なかは狭苦しい、薄汚い部屋で、切り出したままの材木や壊れた家具がそ

wood and broken furniture. A log burning in ❶the fireplace was the only source of light, ❷by which I could make out a number of ❸hunched figures ❹sitting around the room. The old man led me to a chair beside the fire with ❺a grudgingness that suggested it was the very one he had just ❻vacated. Once I sat down, I found I could not easily turn my head to see my ❼surroundings or the others in the room. But the warmth of the fire was very ❽welcome, and for a moment I just stared into its flames, ❾a pleasant grogginess drifting over me. Voices came from behind me, ❿inquiring if I was well, if I had come far, if I was hungry, and I replied ⓫as best I could, though I was aware that my answers were ⓬barely adequate. ⓭Eventually, the questions ⓮ceased, and it occurred to me that my presence was creating a heavy ⓯awkwardness, but I was so ⓰grateful for the warmth and the chance to rest that I

❶ the fireplace: 暖炉
❷ by which I could make out ...: その光源を頼りに〜が見えた。make out は暗くて見にくいものや、乱暴で読みにくい字などが、見える、読めるといったときに使う。*I can't make out this handwriting.*（こんな筆跡、読めない）
❸ hunched: 背を丸めて
❹ sitting around the room: around はある場所の外周を意味することもあれば、（この場合のように）内周を意味することもある。walk around the house といえば、どちらの意味にもなりうる。どちらであるかは、ほとんどの場合文脈から判断できる。
❺ a grudgingness: しぶしぶの態度
❻ vacate(d):（席などを）空ける
❼ surroundings: 周囲
❽ welcome: うれしい、有難い
❾ a pleasant grogginess drifting over me: 直訳は「快いふらふらの感覚（grogginess）が私の上に漂ってきて（drifiting）」。

こら中に転がっていた。暖炉で燃えている一本の丸太が唯一の光源で、その光を頼りに見てみると、背を丸めた人影がいくつか、部屋のあちこちに散らばっているのがわかった。老人は私を暖炉のそばの椅子に案内したが、その不承不承の様子から、それはついいままで自分が座っていた椅子だと思われた。いったん腰掛けてしまうと首が思うように動かせず、自分の周りやほかの連中を見るのは容易でなくなった。けれども暖炉の暖かさは実に心地よく、少しのあいだ私はただぼんやりと炎を眺め、快い疲労感に見舞われるままにしていた。背後から何人かの声がして、元気かい、遠くから来たのか、腹は減っていないかと訊いてくれており、私としても精一杯答えはしたが、その返答がおよそ十分でないことは自覚していた。やがて質問も止み、自分がそこにいるせいで重々しいぎこちなさが生じていることを私は感じとったが、とにかく暖かいことと、体を休められることが心底有難く、それもろくに気にな

❿ inquiring <inquire: ～を訊ねる
⓫ as best I could: できる限り、精一杯
⓬ barely adequate: かろうじて要件を満たして
⓭ Eventually: 英和辞典には「結局、ついに」といった訳語が載っているが、「やがて」あたりが妥当なことも多いように思う。中村保男は「私はこの語をよく『ゆくゆくは』と訳している」と述べていて（『新装版　英和翻訳表現辞典』）、文脈によってはたしかにこれも適切である。
⓮ cease(d): 終わる、止む
⓯ (an) awkwardness: ぎこちない雰囲気
⓰ grateful: 感謝して

❶hardly cared.

❷Nonetheless, when the silence behind me ❸had gone unbroken for several minutes, I ❹resolved to address my hosts with a little more civility, and I ❺turned in my chair. It was then, ❻as I did so, that I ❼was suddenly seized by an intense sense of recognition. I had chosen the cottage ❽quite at random, but now I could see that it was ❾none other than the very one in which I had spent my years in this village. My ❿gaze moved immediately to ⓫the far corner—at this moment ⓬shrouded in darkness—to the spot that had been *my* corner, where once my mattress had been and where I had spent many ⓭tranquil hours ⓮browsing through books or ⓯conversing with whoever happened to drift in. On summer days, the windows, and often the door, were left open to ⓰allow a refreshing breeze to blow right through. ⓱Those were the days when the cottage was surrounded by open fields and there

❶ hardly cared: ほとんどどうでもよかった

❷ Nonetheless: それでもなお。nevertheless と同じと考えてさしつかえない。

❸ had gone unbroken for several minutes: 数分とぎれず続いていた

❹ resolved to address my host with a little more civility: 直訳は「もう少しの礼儀（civility）をもってわが接待主たち（hosts）に向かって話そう（address）と決心した（resolved）」。

❺ turned in my chair: 直訳は「椅子の中で体を回した」。座った人間が何らかのやり方で動く、ということを言うとき、英語ではこのin my chairのように、「座ったまま」ということを律儀に言い添えるのが普通。

❻ as I did so: そうするさなかに（as I turned in my chair）

❼ was suddenly seized by an intense sense of recognition: 直訳は「強い認識の感覚に突如襲われた」。recognition については p. 184, l. 8 と p. 188, l. 11 の註を参照。

❽ quite at random: まったくランダムに、無作為に

らなかった。

とはいえ、背後の沈黙が数分間とぎれずに続くと、さすがに私ももう少し礼を示さねばと思って、座ったままうしろに向き直った。と、ちょうどそのとき、一気に記憶がよみがえってきた。私としてはまったく行きあたりばったりにこのコテージを選んだつもりでいたのだが、実はここそ、自分がこの村で数年間を過ごした家だったことがわかったのである。私のまなざしは、ただちに奥の一角へと向けられた——目下のところ闇に包まれている、かつて私の一角だった、私のマットレスが置かれていた場所へと。あそこで私は、本をぱらぱら読んだり、たまたま入ってきた者とお喋りに興じたりして、何時間も穏やかな時を過ごしたものだった。夏になると窓が開けられ、しばしば玄関の扉も開けられて、気持ちのよいそよ風が吹き抜けていった。あのこ

❾ none other than ...: 〜にほかならない、まさに〜だ
❿ (a) gaze: 凝視、視線
⓫ the far corner: 奥の隅
⓬ shroud(ed): 〜を覆う、包む
⓭ tranquil: 穏やかな
⓮ browsing <browse:（本などを）拾い読みする
⓯ conversing with whoever happened to drift in: 誰であれふらっと入ってきた人間と会話して
⓰ allow a refreshing breeze to blow right through: すがすがしい微風を通り抜けさせる。right は p. 166, l. 13 と同様。
⓱ Those were the days when ...: 当時は〜したものだった

would come from outside the voices of my friends, ❶lazing in the long grass, ❷arguing over poetry or philosophy. These precious ❸fragments of the past came back to me so powerfully that ❹it was all I could do not to ❺make straight for my old corner ❻then and there.

Someone was speaking to me again, perhaps asking another question, but I hardly listened. Rising, I ❼peered through the shadows into my corner, and could now ❽make out a narrow bed, covered by an old curtain, ❾occupying more or less the exact space where my mattress had been. The bed looked extremely ❿inviting, and I found myself ⓫cutting into something the old man was saying.

'⓬Look,' I said, 'I know this is a bit ⓭blunt. But, you see, I've come such a long way today. I really need to lie down, close my eyes, even if it's just for a few minutes. After that, I'm happy to ⓮talk all you like.'

❶ lazing <laze: のらくら過ごす
❷ arguing over poetry or philosophy: argue は「喧嘩する」「口論する」と訳した方が適切なことも多いが、ここは「議論を戦わす」といった響き。
❸ fragment(s): 断片、かけら
❹ it was all I could do not to ...: 〜しないだけで（〜せぬようこらえるので）精一杯だった
❺ make straight for ...: 〜へ一直線に向かう
❻ then and there: その時そこで。here and now（いまここで）を過去にすると、このように「時間」と「場所」の順番が入れ替わる。
❼ peered through the shadows into my corner: 目を凝らして、影の向こうの、（かつての）私の場所を見ようとした
❽ make out a narrow bed: make out は p. 194, l. 2 に同じ。

ろコテージの周りは一面の野原で、背の高い草にのんびり埋もれた友人たちが詩や哲学を論じる声が聞こえてきたものだ。こうした過去の愛おしいかけらが、あまりにも生々しく戻ってきたものだから、即座にかつてのわが居場所に飛んで行かぬよう自分を抑えるにも一苦労だった。

ふたたび誰かが私に声をかけていた。また何か訊ねているのだろうが、私はろくに聞いていなかった。立ち上がって、影の向こうのわが一角を覗いてみると、細長いベッドが見えた。古いカーテンが掛けてあって、かつて私のマットレスがあったのとほぼ同じ位置に置いてある。ベッドはものすごく誘惑的に見え、私は老人が何か言っているところに思わず割って入ってしまった。

「あの、ちょっと礼儀知らずかもしれないけど」と私は言った。「でもとにかく、今日は遠くから来たもので。少しでいいから、横になって目を閉じたいんだ。そのあとでいくらでも話しますから」

❾ occupy(ing):（場所などを）占める
❿ inviting: 誘惑的な
⓫ cutting into something the old man was saying: 老人が言っている何かに割って入って
⓬ Look: ねえ、あのさ。丁寧な言い方とは言いかねる。
⓭ blunt: 無遠慮な、ぶしつけな
⓮ talk all you like: あなた方が好きなだけ話をする

I could see the figures around the room ❶shifting uneasily. Then a new voice said, rather sullenly, '❷Go ahead then. Have ❸a nap. ❹Don't mind us.'

But I was already ❺picking my way through the clutter toward my corner. The bed ❻felt damp, and the springs ❼creaked under my weight, but ❽no sooner had I curled up with my back to the room than ❾my many hours of travelling began to catch up with me. As I was ❿drifting off, I heard the old man saying, '⓫It's Fletcher, all right. God, he's ⓬aged.'

A woman's voice said, 'Should we let him go to sleep like that? He might wake in a few hours and then we'll have to ⓭stay up with him.'

'Let him sleep for an hour or so,' someone else said. 'If he's still asleep after an hour, we'll wake him.'

At this point, ⓮sheer exhaustion overtook me.

*

❶ shift(ing): そわそわ動く、もぞもぞする

❷ Go ahead: 好きにするがいい

❸ a nap: ひと眠り

❹ Don't mind us: 私たちのことは気にしなくていい

❺ picking my way through the clutter: 物がごちゃごちゃあるなか（the clutter）を、かき分けるように進んで

❻ felt damp:「湿っているように感じられた」というより、「触れると湿っていた」というふうに、feel は「触覚」を強調して訳すべき場合が多い。

❼ creak(ed): きしむ

❽ no sooner had I curled up with my back to the room than ...: 部屋に背を向けて丸くなるや否や～した。No sooner had A done B than C did D で As soon as A did B, C did D とほぼ同じ（A が B するや否や C が D した）。

部屋中の人影がそわそわ落着かなげに動くのが見えた。やがて、いままで黙っていた人物の、いささかむすっとした声が言った。「じゃあそうすればいい。一眠りしなよ。私らには構わんでいいから」

だが私はもうすでに､ガラクタをかき分けてわが一角へ向かっていた。ベッドは湿っていたし、スプリングは体の重みでぎしぎし鳴ったが、部屋に背を向けて身を丸めたとたん、長時間旅をしてきた疲れが一気に襲ってきた。うとうとしかけるなかで、老人が「本当にフレッチャーなんだな。いやあ、老けたなあ」と言っているのが聞こえた。

女の声が言った。「あんなふうに寝かせちゃっていいの？　何時間かしたら起きてきて、私たち一緒に起きてなきゃいけなくなるかも」

「一時間かそこら寝かせておくさ」とほかの誰かが言った。「一時間経っても眠っていたら起こそう」

この時点で、全面的な疲労が私を包んだ。

＊

❾ my many hours of travelling began to catch up with me: 直訳は「長時間の旅が私に追いついてきはじめた」。

❿ drift(ing) off: うとうと眠りに落ちる

⓫ It's Fletcher, all right: all right は、フレッチャーじゃないように見えるがやっぱりフレッチャーだ、という含み。

⓬ age(d): 老ける

⓭ stay up: 眠らずに起きている

⓮ sheer exhaustion overtook me: 直訳は「芯からの疲労が私に追いついた」。l. 7 の catch up を引き継いで、ここでは overtook（<overtake）という、より「追いついた感」が強い言葉に変わっている。

It was not a continuous or comfortable sleep. I ❶drifted between sleep and waking, always conscious of voices behind me in the room. At some point, I was aware of a woman saying, '❷I don't know how I was ever under his spell. He looks such ❸a ragamuffin now.'

In my state of near-sleep, I ❹debated with myself whether these words ❺applied to me or, perhaps, to David Maggis, but before long sleep ❻engulfed me once more.

When I next awoke, the room appeared to have ❼grown both darker and colder. Voices were continuing behind me in lowered tones, but I could make no sense of the conversation. I now ❽felt embarrassed at having gone to sleep in the way I had, and ❾for a few further moments remained motionless with my face to the wall. But ❿something about me must have revealed that I was awake, ⓫for a woman's voice, ⓬breaking off from the general conversation, said, 'Oh, look, look.' Some whispers were

❶ drifted between sleep and waking: 眠りと目覚めのあいだをさまよった
❷ I don't know how I was ever under his spell: 彼の虜になったことがあったなんて信じられない。under one's spell で「～に呪縛されて」。
❸ a ragamuffin: ぼろを着た人
❹ debated with myself whether ...: ～かどうか自問した
❺ applied to <apply to ...: ～に当てはまる
❻ engulf(ed): ～を呑み込む
❼ grow(n): (温度や明るさに関して) ～になる。*It grew hotter and hotter.* (どんどん暑くなった)
❽ felt embarrassed: 気まずい思いだった
❾ for a few further moments: まだしばらく
❿ something about me must have revealed that ...: 直訳は「私の何かが、

それは持続する快い眠りではなかった。私はうとうとと寝たり起きたりをくり返し、背後の部屋で発せられる声をつねに意識していた。ある時点で、一人の女がこう言うのが耳に入った――「何であんな人に夢中になったのかわからないわ。いまじゃまるで浮浪者じゃない」

半睡状態のなか、この言葉が私を指したものか、それともデイヴィッド・マギスのことを言っているのか考えてみたが、まもなく眠りがもう一度私を包み込んだ。

次に目ざめると、部屋はさっきより暗く、寒くなったように思えた。人々の声は相変わらず背後で低く続いていたが、話の中身まではわからなかった。あんなふうに寝入ってしまったことがいまとなっては恥ずかしく思えて、私はそのまましばらく、壁に顔を向けたままじっとしていた。が、目ざめたことが何となく伝わってしまったのだろう、みんなの会話を一人の女がさえぎって、「あ、ほら見て、あれ」と言った。ひそひそ声がしばし交わされたのち、

〜ということを明かしたにちがいない」。

⓫ for a woman's voice ...: この for は「というのも〜」「なぜなら〜」の意。

⓬ breaking off from the general conversation: 全体の会話から抜け出て

exchanged, then I heard the sound of someone coming toward my corner. I felt a hand placed gently on my shoulder, and ❶looked up to find a woman kneeling over me. ❷I did not turn my body sufficiently to see the room, but I got the impression that it ❸was lit by dying embers, and the woman's face was visible only in shadow.

'Now, Fletcher,' she said. '❹It's time we had a talk. I've waited a long time for you to come back. I've thought about you often.'

I ❺strained to see her more clearly. She was somewhere in her forties, and even in the ❻gloom I noticed a sleepy sadness in her eyes. But her face failed to ❼stir in me even the ❽faintest of memories.

'I'm sorry,' I said. 'I have no ❾recollection of you. But please forgive me if we met some time ago. I do get very disoriented these days.'

'Fletcher,' she said, 'when we used to know one another, I

❶ looked up to find a woman kneeling over me: 顔を上げたら、一人の女がひざまずいてこっちを見下ろしてい（るのが見え）た。この to find ... という不定詞は「結果」（〜したら〜する）の用法。
❷ I did not turn my body sufficiently to ...: 〜するに十分なほど体を回しはしなかった
❸ was lit by dying embers: 消えかけの残り火で照らされていた
❹ It's time we had a talk: 私たちが話をすべき時だ。It's time+ 過去形で「もう〜していい時だ」。
❺ strain(ed): 目を凝らす
❻ gloom: 薄暗がり
❼ stir:（記憶などを）呼び起こす
❽ faint(est): かすかな

誰かがこっちへやって来る音が聞こえた。片手がそっと肩に置かれるのを感じて顔を上げると、一人の女がかがみ込んで私を見下ろしていた。私は部屋が見えるほど大きく体を動かしはしなかったが、あたりは暖炉の残り火で照らされているようだった。女の顔は影しか見えなかった。

「ねえ、フレッチャー」と彼女は言った。「あたしたち、話すべきだと思うの。あなたが帰ってくるのを、あたし長いあいだ待っていたのよ。あなたのこと何度も考えていたのよ」

女をもっとはっきり見ようと、私は目を凝らした。歳は40代、薄闇のなかでもその目に浮かぶ眠たげな悲哀が見てとれた。でもその顔を見ても、何の記憶もよみがえってこなかった。

「申し訳ないが、あなたのことは覚えていないんだ」と私は言った。「でも以前知り合いだったなら許してほしい。このごろはすごく混乱してしまうもので」

「フレッチャー」と女は言った。「あたしたちが知り合いだったころ、あた

❾ (a) recollection: 記憶

was young and beautiful. I ❶idolized you, and everything you said seemed like an answer. ❷Now here you are, back again. I've wanted to tell you for many years that you ❸ruined my life.'

'❹You're being unfair. All right, I was mistaken about a lot of things. But I never ❺claimed to have any answers. All I said in those days was that it was our duty, all of us, to ❻contribute to the debate. We knew so much more about the issues than the ordinary people here. If people like us ❼procrastinated, claiming we didn't yet know enough, ❽then who was there to act? But I never claimed I had the answers. No, you're being unfair.'

'Fletcher,' she said, and her voice was ❾oddly gentle, 'you used to ❿make love to me, ⓫more or less every time I wandered in here to your room. In this corner, we did all kinds of beautifully ⓬dirty things. It's odd to think ⓭how I could have once been so physically excited by you. And here you're just ⓮a foul-smelling bundle of rags now. But look at me—I'm still attractive. My face has got a

❶ idolize(d): ～を偶像視する、崇拝する
❷ Now here you are, back again: そんなあなたが、ここに戻ってきた
❸ ruin(ed): ～を台なしにする
❹ You're being unfair: You're unfairと違って、いつもそうだというのではなく、いまのその発言は不当だ、という含み。
❺ claim(ed): ～を主張する。日本語の「クレーム」には「文句」のニュアンスがついて回るが、claim は「主張」「要求」を意味する語。すぐあと l. 8 の claiming も同様（「クレーム」はむしろ complaint）。
❻ contribute to the debate: 討論に貢献する。この the debate とは何なのか、あるいは次行の the issues（論点）とは何なのかは最後まで明らかにされないが、たとえば 1960 年代の学生運動の背後にあった政治論争のようなものを想像すればいいだろう（もちろん、この作品を、60 年代とその後をめぐる寓話という

しは若くて綺麗だった。あたしはあなたを崇拝して、あなたが言うことは何でも正しい答えだと思えた。そしていま、あなたは戻ってきた。もう何年も前から言いたかったのよ、あなたがあたしの人生を滅茶苦茶にしたってことを」

「それは不当な批判だよ。たしかに私は、いろんなことについて間違った考えを抱いていた。でも、正しい答えを持っていると主張したことは一度もない。あのころ私が言ったのは、論争に貢献するのが我々の義務だ、我々みんなの義務だ、ということに尽きる。我々はここに住む普通の人たちよりも、問題についてずっとよく知っている。もし我々のような者が、まだ十分に知らないからなどと言ってぐずぐずしていたら、いったい誰が行動する？　そう言ったんだよ。答えを持っているなどと言った覚えはない。それは不当な批判だ」

「フレッチャー」と女は言った。妙に優しい声だった。「あなたはいつも私を愛したのよ、あたしがこの部屋に訪ねてくるとほとんどいつもね。この一角で、あたしたちはありとあらゆる素敵にいやらしいことをしたわ。あなたにあんなに激しく体が興奮させられたかと思うと、妙な気持ちになるわ。いまのあなたは、嫌な臭(にお)いのする襤褸(ぼろ)切れの束。でもあたしを見てよ――あた

ふうに限定するのはよくないが)。

❼ procrastinate(d): ぐずぐずして何もしない

❽ then who was there to act?: だとしたら、誰が行動するというのか？ then は「そのとき」ではなく「それなら」。

❾ oddly: 奇妙に

❿ make love to ...: ～と性交する（比較的無難な言い方)。

⓫ more or less every time: ほぼ毎回

⓬ dirty: 淫らな

⓭ how I could have ...: いったいどうして～したのか（自分でもわからない、という含み)。

⓮ a foul-smelling bundle of rags: 嫌な臭いのする襤褸切れの束

bit lined, but when I walk in the village streets I wear dresses I've made specially to ❶show off my figure. A lot of men want me still. But you, no woman would look at you now. A bundle of ❷stinking rags and ❸flesh.'

'I don't remember you,' I said. 'And I've no time for sex these days. I've other things to worry about. More serious things. ❹Very well, I was mistaken about a lot in those days. But I've done more than most to ❺try and make amends. You see, even now I'm travelling. I've never stopped. I've travelled and travelled ❻trying to undo what damage I may once have caused. ❼That's more than can be said of some others from those days. ❽I bet Maggis, for instance, ❾hasn't worked nearly as hard to try and put things right.'

The woman was stroking my hair.

'Look at you. I used to do this, ❿run my fingers through your hair. Look at ⓫this filthy mess. I'm sure you're ⓬contaminated

❶ show off ...: ～を見せびらかす
❷ stinking: 悪臭のする
❸ flesh:（人間や動物の）肉。基本的には、骨と皮を除いた部分を指すが、ここでは大まかに「肉体」の意。
❹ Very well ...:「そう、たしかに……」の意なので、まず間違いなくそのあとに but が来る。
❺ try and make amends: 埋め合わせようと努める。try and ... は try to ... とそんなに変わらない。
❻ trying to undo what damage I may once have caused: 私がかつて起こしたかもしれない害を帳消しにしようと。the damage でなく what damage と言い、I once caused ではなく I may once have caused と言うことによって、自分が害を引き起こしたという事実を曖昧に響かせようという（ほとんど無意識にはたらいている）意図が透けて見える。

しはまだ魅力的よ。顔は少し皺になったけど、村の通りを歩くときは体形を見せつけるよう自分で作ったドレスを着るのよ。あたしを求める男はまだ大勢いる。でもあなたは、もういまのあなたに目を向ける女なんていやしない。ぷんぷん臭う、襤褸切れと肉の束よ」

「君のことは覚えていないんだ」と私は言った。「それにこのごろはもうセックスに用はない。心配すべきことはほかにあるからね、もっと真面目なことが。結構、たしかにあのころ私はいろんなことについて間違っていた。でも私は、たいていの人間以上にその埋め合わせに努めてきたつもりだ。いいかい、私はいまでも旅をしているんだ。立ち止まったことは一度もない。旅をずっとずっと続けて、かつて引き起こしたかもしれない害を帳消しにしようとしているんだ。あのころの連中で、そこまでやっている人間はそういないと思うね。たとえばマギスなんか、とうてい私ほど物事を正そうと頑張っているとは思えないね」

女は私の髪を撫でていた。

「いまのあなたと来たら。あたしは前にもよくこうしたのよ、こうやってあなたの髪を指で撫でたのよ。見てよ、この汚(きたな)らしいかたまり。あなたきっと、

❼ That's more than can be said of ...: それは〜について言える以上のことだ＝〜についてそんなことは言えない。That's more than you can say about ... と言うのとだいたい同じ。

❽ I bet: I'm sure

❾ hasn't worked nearly as hard: とうていそんなに懸命に頑張ってはいない。not ... nearly は「それほど〜ではない」という弱い否定ではなく、「とうてい〜ではない」という強い否定。

❿ run my fingers through your hair: あなたの髪に指を滑らせる＝あなたの髪を撫でる

⓫ this filthy mess: この不潔な、見苦しいもの

⓬ contaminated with: 〜に汚染されて、たかられて

with all sorts of ❶parasites.' But she continued slowly to run her fingers through the dirty ❷knots. I failed to feel anything erotic from this, as perhaps she wished me to do. Rather, her ❸caresses felt ❹maternal. Indeed, for a moment it was as though I had finally reached ❺some cocoon of protectiveness, and I began once more to feel sleepy. But suddenly she stopped and ❻slapped me hard on the forehead.

'❼Why don't you join the rest of us now? You've had your sleep. ❽You've got a lot of explaining to do.' With that she got up and left.

For the first time, I turned my body sufficiently to survey the room. I saw the woman ❾making her way past the clutter on the floor, then sitting down in a rocking chair by the fireplace. I could see three other figures hunched around the dying fire. ❿One I recognised to be the old man who had opened the door. The two others—sitting together on what looked like a wooden ⓫trunk—

❶ parasite(s): 寄生虫
❷ knot(s):（髪の毛などの）もつれ
❸ caress(es): 愛撫 /kərés/
❹ maternal: 母性的な
❺ some cocoon of protectiveness: 直訳は「何らかの、保護性を有する繭」。
❻ slap(ped): ～を平手で打つ、ひっぱたく
❼ Why don't you join the rest of us now?: p. 192, l. 3 と同じで、「なぜ～しないのか」と問うているのではない。
❽ You've got a lot of explaining to do: あなたには説明すべきことがたくさんある。*You have a lot to answer for.*（あなたには責任をとるべきことがたくさんある＝あなたには大いに責任がある）などと同じ。
❾ making her way past the clutter: p. 200, l. 4 の 'picking my way

いろんな虫にたかられてるわね」。しかし女はなおも、汚いもつれ髪にゆっくり指を滑らせていた。私をエロチックな気持ちにさせたいのかもしれないが、全然そんな気分にはなれなかった。むしろその愛撫は母性的に感じられた。実際、一瞬のあいだ、やっとのことで自分を守ってくれる繭（まゆ）のようなものにたどり着いた気がして、私はまた眠くなってきた。だが女はいきなり手を止め、私の額を思いきりひっぱたいた。
「さあ、あたしたちのいる方にいらっしゃい。もう十分寝たでしょう。あなた、釈明しなくちゃいけないことがたくさんあるのよ」。そう言って女は腰を上げ、立ち去った。

ここで初めて、私は十分に体を回して室内を見渡した。床に転がったガラクタのあいだを女が縫うように進んで、暖炉のそばの揺り椅子に腰を下ろすのが見えた。消えかけた火の周りにほかにも三人が背を丸めているのが見えた。一人は扉を開けてくれた老人だと知れた。ほか二人は女性で、大きな木箱とおぼしきものに一緒に腰掛けていて、私と話した女とおおよそ同い歳に

through the clutter' と同様。
❿ One I recognised to be ...: 一人は〜だと認識した、わかった
⓫ (a) trunk: 大型の木箱、チェスト

seemed to be women of around the same age as the one who had spoken to me.

The old man noticed that I had turned, and he ❶indicated to the others that I was watching. The four of them ❷proceeded to sit ❸stiffly, not speaking. ❹From the way they did this, it was clear that they had been discussing me ❺thoroughly while I was asleep. In fact, as I watched them I could more or less guess ❻the whole shape their conversation had taken. I could see, for instance, that they had spent some time expressing ❼concern for the young girl I had met outside, and about the effect I might have on her ❽peers.

'They're all so ❾impressionable,' the old man would have said. 'And I heard her inviting him to visit them.'

To which, no doubt, one of the women on the trunk would have said, 'But he can't do much harm now. In our time, we ❿were all taken in because all his kind—they were young and ⓫glamorous. But these days ⓬the odd one passing through from time to time,

❶ indicate(d): (身振りなどで) ～を伝える
❷ proceed(ed): to continue
❸ stiffly: ぎこちなく
❹ From the way they did this: 彼らがこれをしたやり方から＝その様子から見て
❺ thoroughly: 徹底的に
❻ the whole shape their conversation had taken: 彼らの会話が取った全体の形＝会話が始めから終わりまでどう進んだか
❼ concern: 懸念
❽ peer(s): 仲間。たとえば大学の同級生のように、ある程度同じ境遇を共有している仲間を言う。
❾ impressionable: 影響されやすい

見えた。

私がこっちを向いたことに気がつくと、老人は私が見ていることを仲間に合図で知らせた。四人はぎこちなく座ったまま何も言わなかった。その雰囲気からして、眠っているあいだにみんなで私のことを徹底的に話しあっていたのは明らかだった。そればかりか、そうやって彼らを見ていると、会話がどう展開したか、ほぼすべて見当がついた。たとえば、私が外で会った若い娘について、そして彼女の仲間に私が及ぼしかねない影響について、しばらくのあいだみんなで不安を表明しあったことが私にはわかった。

「みんなすごく感化されやすいからなあ」と老人は言ったことだろう。「奴をコテージに誘っているのも聞いたぞ」

それを受けて、木箱に座った女の一方がきっとこう言ったことだろう。「でもいまのあの人に大した害は及ぼせやしないわよ。あたしたちが若かったころみんなだまされたのは、あの連中が——あいつらが若くて華やかだったからよ。でもこのごろじゃ、たまに一人村を通りかかっても、あんなふうによぼよぼで、くたびれ切っていて——むしろ逆に、あのころの神話を壊し

❿ were all taken in: だまされた
⓫ glamorous: 華やかな
⓬ the odd one passing through from time to time: 時おり（from time to time）通りかかる（passing through）半端な一人二人（the odd one）

looking all ❶decrepit and burned out ❷like that—if anything, it ❸goes to demystify all that talk about the old days. In any case, people like him have changed their position so much these days. They don't know themselves what they believe.'

The old man would have shaken his head. 'I saw the way that young girl was looking at him. ❹All right, he looks a ❺pitiful mess over there just now. But ❻once his ego's fed a little, once he ❼has the flattery of the young people, sees how they want to hear his ideas, then ❽there'll be no stopping him. It'll be just like before. He'll ❾have them all working for his ❿causes. Young girls like that, ⓫there's so little for them to believe in now. Even ⓬a stinking tramp like this could give them a purpose.'

Their conversation, all the time I slept, ⓭would have gone something very much like that. But now, as I observed them from my corner, they continued to sit in ⓮guilty silence, staring at the last of their fire. After a while, I rose to my feet. ⓯Absurdly,

❶ decrepit and burned out: よぼよぼで、燃え尽きて
❷ like that: 眠っているフレッチャーの方を指さすか、見るかしている。
❸ goes to demystify all that talk about the old days: 昔についてのいろんな話を脱神話化するのに役立つ。go to ... は何かを明かしたり示したりするのに「役立つ」という意。*This goes to show how stupid people can be.*（世の中の人がいかに愚かになりうるか、ここからもわかる）
❹ All right ...: まあたしかに〜。p. 208, ll. 6-7 の 'Very well ...' と同じに、聴き手はこのあとに but ... と来るのを予期しながら聴くことになる。
❺ pitiful: みじめな
❻ once his ego's fed a little: ひとたびエゴがいくらか満たされたら（once his ego is fed a little)。fed <feed: 〜に滋養を与える、満足させる
❼ has the flattery of the young people: 若者の賛辞を受ける

てくれるくらい。そもそも近ごろはあの連中もずいぶん立場を変えたし。自分が何を信じているのか、本人たちもわかっちゃいないのよ」

老人は首を横に振ったことだろう。「あの若い娘が奴を見る目つきを見たんだ。そう、いまはたしかに、あそこに転がってる姿は哀れもいいところだ。だがひとたびうぬぼれを少しばかり満たしてもらって、若い連中にちやほやされて、みんなが自分の思想を聞きたがってると思ったら、もう手が付けられなくなるぞ。前とまったく同じになる。みんなを自分の大義のために働かせるようになってしまう。ああいう若い娘たちは、今日(こんにち)信じられるものがほとんど何もないんだ。こいつみたいなプンプン臭う流れ者だって、あの子たちに目的を与えられるんだ」

私がずっと眠っているあいだ、彼らの会話はほぼそんなふうに進んでいったことだろう。だがいま、わが一角から私が見守るなか、彼らは依然やましげな沈黙を保って、ほぼ燃えつきた火をじっと見ていた。少しして、私は立ち上がった。馬鹿げたことに、四人は私から目をそらしたままだ。誰か何か

❽ there'll be no stopping him: 彼を止めようはないだろう。There is no ...ing で「～しようはない」。
❾ have them all working: 彼らみんなを働かせる
❿ cause(s): 運動などの統一目標、看板として掲げられた大きな目的のこと。
⓫ there's so little for them to believe in now: 今日、彼らが信じられるものはほとんどない。believe in ... はこの場合「～の価値を信じる」。p. 142, 註❶を参照。
⓬ a stinking tramp: 悪臭のする浮浪者
⓭ would have gone something very much like that: ほとんどそういうように進んだことだろう
⓮ guilty: やましい
⓯ absurdly: 馬鹿げたことに

the four of them ❶kept their gazes averted from me. I waited a few moments to see if any of them would say anything. Finally, I said, 'All right, I was asleep earlier, but I've guessed what you were saying. Well, ❷you'll be interested to know I'm going to do the very thing you feared. I'm going this moment to the young people's cottage. I'm going to tell them what to do with all their energy, all their dreams, ❸their urge to achieve something of lasting good in this world. Look at you, what ❹a pathetic bunch. Crouching in your cottage, afraid to do anything, afraid of me, of Maggis, of anyone else from those times. Afraid to do anything in ❺the world out there, just because once we made a few mistakes. Well, those young people ❻haven't yet sunk so low, despite all ❼the lethargy you've been ❽preaching at them ❾down the years. I'll talk to them. I'll ❿undo in half an hour all of your ⓫sorry efforts.'

'You see,' the old man said to the others. 'I knew it would be this way. We ought to stop him, but what can we do?'

❶ kept their gazes averted: 眼差しをそむけつづけた
❷ you'll be interested to know ...: 直訳は「～と知ったら君たちは興味深く思うだろう」だが、せいぜい「お伝えしておくが」「言っておくがな」という程度。
❸ their urge to achieve something of lasting good: 永続する善（lasting good）を何かしら成し遂げたいという欲求（urge）
❹ a pathetic bunch: 情けない一団
❺ the world out there: 外に広がっている世界、外の世界
❻ haven't yet sunk so low: 直訳は「まだそこまで低く沈んでいない」。
❼ the lethargy: 無気力、怠惰
❽ preach(ing): ～を説く
❾ down the years: 長年のあいだに
❿ undo: ～を元に戻す、～がなかったような状態にする

言うかと思って、しばらく待ってみた。結局私が先に口を開いた。「結構、さっきは眠ってたけど君たちの話は見当がついたよ。お知らせしておこう、私は君らがまさに恐れていることをやるつもりだ。いまからすぐ、若者たちのコテージに行く。彼らの持っているエネルギー、夢、何かこの世界で永続的な善をなし遂げたいという欲求、そういうものをどう使ったらいいか教えてやるつもりだ。君たちのていたらくを見ろ、みんな何て情けない有様だ。小屋にこもって、何をする勇気もなく、私を怖がり、マギスを、あのころの人間みんなを怖がり、外の世界で何をするのも怖がっている、それも単に、かつて私たちがいくつか過ちを犯したからというだけの理由で。だが、あの若い連中はそこまで堕(お)ちちゃいない、君たちに長年さんざん無気力を吹き込まれてきたにもかかわらずね。私は彼らに話をする。君たちの情けない努力の成果を、30分でぶち壊してやる」

「ほら、言っただろう」と老人は仲間たちに言った。「わかっていたんだ、こうなることは。こいつを止めなくちゃいかん、だが私らに何ができる？」

⓫ sorry: みじめな、情けない

I ❶crashed my way across the room, picked up my bag, and went out into the night.

The girl was still standing outside when I emerged. ❷She seemed to be expecting me and with a nod began to lead the way.

The night was ❸drizzly and dark. We ❹twisted and turned along the narrow paths that ❺ran between the cottages. Some of the cottages we passed looked so ❻decayed and crumbling that I felt I could destroy one of them simply by running at it with all my weight.

The girl kept ❼a few paces ahead, ❽occasionally ❾glancing back at me over her shoulder. Once she said, 'Wendy's going to be so pleased. She was sure it was you when you went past earlier. ❿By now, she'll have guessed she was right, ⓫because I've been away this long, and she'll have brought ⓬the whole crowd together. They'll all be waiting.'

❶ crashed my way across the room:（物を壊さんばかりの勢いで）入口の方まで行った。p. 200, l. 4 の 'picking my way through the clutter' に較べてずいぶん威勢がよくなっている。

❷ She seemed to be expecting me:（当然のごとく）私を待っていたふうだった

❸ drizzly: 霧雨の降る

❹ twisted and turned: twist and turn は「しきりに寝返りを打つ」という意味になったりもするが、ここではさんざん曲がりくねった道を進んでいったということ。

❺ ran between the cottages: 道がいかにも狭くて、両側からコテージが迫っている感じ。

❻ decayed and crumbling: 朽ちて、ぼろぼろ崩れかけている

私は荒々しい足どりで部屋の向こう側まで行き、鞄を手にとって夜のなかに出ていった。

私が出ていくと、娘は依然外に立っていた。私を待っていたのか、軽くうなずいてから先に立って歩き出した。

霧雨の降る、暗い夜だった。両側をコテージにはさまれてくねくね曲がった狭い街路を私たちは進んでいった。通りかかるコテージのいくつかは、すっかり朽ちはて、崩れかけ、力いっぱい体当たりしたら壊れてしまいそうだった。

娘は一貫して何歩か先を行きながら、チラチラ私の方をふり返った。あるとき彼女は言った。「ウェンディ、きっとすごく喜ぶわ。さっき通りかかったときも絶対あなただって言ったのよ。もういまごろは、やっぱりそうだったって思ってるはずよ、あたしがこんなに長く帰ってこないからにはきっとそうだって。仲間も残らず呼んだはずよ。みんな待ってるわ」

「デイヴィッド・マギスのこともこんなふうに歓迎したのかい？」

「ええ、そうよ。あの人が来てあたしたち、すごく興奮したもの」

❼ a few paces: 数歩
❽ occasionally: 時おり
❾ glancing back at me over her shoulder: ちらっと私の方をふり返って。over her shoulder は p. 68, l. 6 の looking over their shoulders と同様。
❿ By now: もう今ごろは
⓫ because I've been away this long: 私がこんなに長く出ている（帰ってこない）から
⓬ the whole crowd: 仲間みんな

'Did you give David Maggis this sort of ❶reception, too?'

'Oh, yes. We were really excited when he came.'

'I'm sure he ❷found that very gratifying. He always ❸had an exaggerated sense of his own importance.'

'Wendy says Maggis was one of the interesting ones, ❹but that you were, well, important. She thinks you were really important.'

I thought about this for a moment.

❺'You know,' I said, 'I've changed my mind on very many things. If Wendy's expecting me to say all the things I used to all those years ago, well, ❻she's going to be in for a disappointment.'

The girl did not seem to hear this, but continued to lead me ❼purposefully through the clusters of cottages.

After a little while, I became aware of footsteps following a dozen or so paces behind us. At first, ❽I assumed this was just some villager out walking and ❾refrained from turning round. But then the girl ❿halted under a street lamp and looked behind us. ⓫I

❶ (a) reception: 歓迎、もてなし

❷ found that very gratifying: そうしてもらってすごく有難く思った。gratifying <gratify: ～を満足させる、有難いという気持ちにさせる

❸ had an exaggerated sense of his own importance: 直訳は「自分の重要性について誇張された感覚を持っていた」。

❹ but that you were, well, important: well と言いよどんだことから、はじめ言おうとした（おそらくはより正直な）言葉は important ほど肯定的ではなかったと思われる。

❺ You know: あのね、いいかい。「君も知っているだろうが」という意味ではない。

❻ she's going to be in for a disappointment: 彼女はがっかりすることになる。to be in for ...: ～を味わうこと必至だ。*If you think this is easy, you're in for a big surprise.*（こんなの簡単だと思ったら大間違いだぜ）

「奴はきっと喜んだろうね。自分の重要さをいつも大きく見過ぎる男だったからな」

「マギスは興味深い人物だってウェンディは言ってるわ、だけどあなたは、ええと、重要だって。あなたはほんとに重要だったってウェンディは言ってる」

そう言われて、私はしばし考えた。

「私もね、いまではすごくいろんなことに関して考えを変えたんだ。もしウェンディが、ずっと昔に私があれこれ言っていたことをもう一度言ってほしいと思ってるんだったら、悪いけどがっかりすると思うね」

娘は私の言葉が聞こえなかったのか、そのままずんずん、立ち並ぶコテージのあいだを進んでいった。

しばらくすると、私たちの十歩ばかりうしろで、もう一人の足音がしていることに私は気がついた。はじめは単に、誰か村人が外に出ているのかと思ってふり返るのも控えていた。だがやがて娘が街灯の下で立ちどまり、うしろを見た。それで私も立ち止まってふり向かざるをえなくなった。黒っぽい外

❼ purposefully: 確固とした様子で、迷わず
❽ I assumed ...: おおかた〜だろうと思った。assume は「〜と思い込む」という意味になることもあるが、ここではそこまで強くない。だがいずれにせよ、根拠なしに推定したり、当然視したりすることをいう。
❾ refrained from turning round: ふり向くことは控えた
❿ halt(ed): 立ち止まる
⓫ I was thus obliged also to ...: かくして（thus）私も〜することを余儀なくされた（obliged）

was thus obliged also to stop and turn. A middle-aged man in ❶a dark overcoat was coming toward us. As he approached, he held out his hand and shook mine, though without smiling.

'❷So,' he said, 'you're here.'

I then realised I knew the man. We had not seen each other since we were ten years old. His name was Roger Button, and he had been in my class at the school I had ❸attended for two years in ❹Canada before my family returned to England. Roger Button and I had not been especially ❺close, but, because he had been a ❻timid boy, and because he, too, was from England, he had for a while ❼followed me about. ❽I had neither seen nor heard from him since that time. Now, as I ❾studied his appearance under the street lamp, I saw ❿the years had not been kind to him. He was bald, his face was ⓫pocked and lined, and there was ⓬a weary sag to his whole ⓭posture. ⓮For all that, there was no mistaking my old classmate.

❶ a dark overcoat: dark という語は「黒っぽい」のみならず濃い色なら茶色でも紺でもよく、かなり範囲が広いので、翻訳者にはなかなか迷惑な言葉である。
❷ So: 日本語の「では」「じゃあ」に近いが、話を切り出す際にほとんど意味なく使われることも多い。
❸ attend(ed):（学校に）通う
❹ Canada: この短篇は冒頭一行目にさっそく England という言葉が出てきて、地理的にけっこう具体的な話かと思いきや、その後場所の固有名詞はまったくなく、ここで久々 Canada と England が出てくるのみである。全体として、イギリスの田舎を彷彿とさせつつ、どこでもありうる場所、どこでもない、「夢の中」の場所についての話という感触が残る。
❺ close: 親しい /klóʊs/
❻ timid: 臆病な
❼ followed me about: 私につきまとった

套を着た中年の男がこっちへやって来る。近づいてきた男は、片手を差し出して私と握手したが、目は笑っていなかった。

「帰ってきたんだな」と男は言った。

そのとき、自分がこの男を知っていることを私は悟った。二人とも10歳だったとき以来、私たちは一度も会っていなかった。男の名はロジャー・バトン、私がカナダの学校に通っていたときの同級生である。私はカナダの学校に二年間通って、それから家族とともにイングランドに戻ったのだった。ロジャー・バトンとは特に親しい仲ではなかったが、彼は臆病な子供だったし、やはりイングランドの生まれだったので、しばらくのあいだ私にくっついて回っていたのだ。あれ以後、私は彼に会いもせず、連絡も受けていなかった。街灯の下でその風貌を吟味してみて、年月が彼を優しく扱ってこなかったことを私は見てとった。頭は禿げ、顔には斑点や皺が浮かび、姿勢全体がくたびれて垂れている感じだ。とはいえ、間違いない、それはかつての級友だった。

❽ I had neither seen nor heard from him: 彼に会ってもいなかったし彼から連絡を受けてもいなかった。seen と heard from が同格。
❾ studied <study: ～をよく見る
❿ the years had not been kind to him: 直訳は「年月は彼に親切でなかった」。
⓫ pocked and lined: あばたや皺がある
⓬ a weary sag: 疲れた感じのたるみ
⓭ posture: 姿勢
⓮ For all that: そういうあれこれはあっても、それにもかかわらず

'Roger,' I said, 'I'm just on my way to visit this young lady's friends. They've gathered together to ❶receive me. ❷Otherwise ❸I'd have come and looked you up ❹straightaway. ❺As it was, ❻I had it in my mind as the next thing to do, even before getting any sleep tonight. I was just thinking to myself, ❼However late things finish at the young people's cottage, ❽I'll go and knock on Roger's door afterward.'

'Don't worry,' said Roger Button as we all started to walk again. 'I know how busy you are. But we ought to talk. ❾Chew over old times. When you last saw me—at school, I mean—I suppose I was ❿a rather feeble specimen. But, you know, ⓫that all changed when I got to fourteen, fifteen. I really ⓬toughened up. Became quite a leader type. But you'd ⓭long since left Canada. I always wondered what would have happened if we'd ⓮come across each other at fifteen. Things would have been ⓯rather different between us, ⓰I

❶ receive me: 私を歓待してくれる
❷ Otherwise: そうでなかったら
❸ I'd have come and looked you up: 君を探しに行ったことだろう。「行った」にあたるところが gone でなく come になっているのは、ロジャーの視点に立っているから。英語は何ごとも自分の視点から話しがちの言語に思えるが、come/go に関しては徹底的に相手の立場に立って言う。
❹ straightaway: ただちに
❺ As it was: 実際は、実のところは
❻ I had it in my mind as ...: それを〜として考えていた
❼ However late: どんなに遅くなっても。自分が考えた（と称している）ことを直接話法的に言っている（そのまま再現している）ので、文の途中だが However と大文字になっている。
❽ I'll go and knock on Roger's door afterward: come/go に関しては徹底的に相手の立場に立つと書いたが、ここでは語り手の頭の中の独り言を（といっ

「ロジャー」と私は言った。「いまちょうど、このお嬢さんのお友だちの家に呼ばれていく途中なんだ。私を歓迎しに、みんなで集まってくれているんだよ。そうでなかったら、すぐにでも君の居所を探したんだが。実際、次はぜひそうしようと思っていたのさ、いっそ今夜寝る前に行こうかってね。ついいまも考えていたのさ、若い人たちのコテージでの用事がどんなに遅くなろうと、それからロジャーを訪ねていこうって」

「気にしなくていい」とロジャーは、三人でまた歩き出すとともに言った。「君が忙しいのは承知している。でも我々は話をしなくちゃいかん。昔のことをじっくり話しあうのさ。君が最後に私を見たとき——つまり学校で一緒だったころの話さ——私は弱々しい、情けない子供だったろうと思う。だけどいいか、私が14、15になるとそれもすっかり変わったんだ。私はすごく強くなった。典型的なリーダー・タイプになったんだよ。でも君はもうずっと前にカナダを去っていた。いつも考えたよ、我々が15のときに出会っていたらどうなっていただろうってね。きっと我々の関係も、相当違ったものになった

ても出任せの作り話だが）再現しているので I'll go ... となっている。

❾ Chew over old times: 昔のことを、とくと話しあう

❿ a rather feeble specimen: 弱々しい奴

⓫ that all changed: それもすべて変わった

⓬ toughened up: 強くなった

⓭ long since: もうずっと前に

⓮ come across ...: 〜に出会う

⓯ rather: 英和辞典には「幾分」とあったり「かなり」とあったり、いったいどのくらいなんだ、と思ってしまうが、まあ「かなり」に近い方が多いように思う。日本語で「ちょっと」と言いながらちょっとどころではない（「ちょっと怒ってるみたいだぜ」）ことに近いか。特に訳さなくてもいいように思える場合もある（たとえば l. 11 の rather）。

⓰ I assure you:「私はあなたに保証する」というより「きっと」に近い。

assure you.'

As he said this, memories ❶came flooding back. In those days, Roger Button had idolized me, and ❷in return I had ❸bullied him ❹incessantly. However, there had existed between us a curious understanding that my bullying him ❺was all for his own good; that when, without warning, I suddenly punched him in the stomach on the playground, or when, passing him in ❻the corridor, I ❼impulsively wrenched his arm up his back until he started to cry, I was doing so in order to help him toughen up. ❽Accordingly, ❾the principal effect such attacks had on our relationship was to ❿keep him in awe of me. This all came back to me as I listened to the weary-looking man walking beside me.

'Of course,' Roger Button ⓫went on, perhaps guessing ⓬my train of thought, '⓭it might well be that if you hadn't treated me the way you did I'd never have become what I did at fifteen. In any case, I've often wondered how it would have been if we'd met just

❶ came flooding back: 洪水のように戻ってきた、生々しくよみがえった
❷ in return: お返しに、それに応えて
❸ bullied <bully: ～をいじめる
❹ incessantly: 絶え間なく
❺ was all for his own good: すべて彼のためだった
❻ the corridor: 廊下
❼ impulsively wrenched his arm up his back: 衝動的に腕を背中でねじり上げた
❽ Accordingly: それゆえ
❾ the principal effect: 主要な効果、主たる結果
❿ keep him in awe of me: 彼が私に畏怖の念を抱きつづける状態に保つ
⓫ went on: 話を続けた

と思うね」

彼がそう言うのを聞いているうちに、記憶が一気によみがえってきた。あのころ、ロジャー・バトンは私を偶像視していた。そして私は、年中彼をいじめていたのだ。しかしながら、私たちのあいだには奇妙な了解のようなものが存在していた。つまり、私が彼をいじめるのも、すべて彼のためなのだと二人とも納得していて、運動場でいきなり彼の腹にパンチを浴びせても、廊下ですれ違いざまに腕を背中でねじり上げて彼が泣き出すまでそうしていても、あくまで彼が強くなるのを助けるためなのだと二人とも承知していたのである。したがって、そのようにいじめることが我々の関係にどう作用したかといえば、何よりもまず、彼が私を畏怖するままでいるという方向に働いたのだ。私と並んで歩く、疲れた様子の男の話を聞きながら、こうしたすべてが戻ってきた。

「まあたしかに」とロジャー・バトンは、私の思考の流れを察したか、話を続けた。「君が私にああいう仕打ちをしなかったら、私も 15 歳になってあんなふうにはならなかったかもしれん。とにかくしじゅう考えたものさ、私たちが数年あとに出会っていたらどうなっていただろうとね。あのころには私

⓬ my train of thought: 私の思考の流れ。「列車」とはずいぶん違う意味に思えるが、「列車」も車両（car）が連なっているから train なのであって、発想は同じ。
⓭ it might well be that ...: ～ということも大いにありうる

a few years later. I really was ❶something to be reckoned with by then.'

We were once again walking along the narrow twisted ❷passages between cottages. The girl was still leading the way, but she was now walking much faster. Often ❸we would only just manage to catch a glimpse of her turning some corner ahead of us, and ❹it struck me that we would have to ❺keep alert if we were not to lose her.

'Today, of course,' Roger Button was saying, '❻I've let myself go a bit. But ❼I have to say, old fellow, you seem to ❽be in much worse shape. ❾Compared with you, I'm an athlete. ❿Not to put too fine a point on it, you're just a filthy old tramp now, really, aren't you? But, you know, for a long time after you left I continued to idolize you. Would Fletcher do this? What would Fletcher think if he saw me doing that? Oh, yes. It was only when I got to fifteen or so that ⓫I looked back on it all and saw through you. Then I was

❶ something to be reckoned with: 侮れない存在（成句）
❷ passage(s): 通路
❸ we would only just manage to catch a glimpse: ちらっと一目見るのがやっとだった
❹ it struck me that ...: 〜だと思いあたった
❺ keep alert: 油断を怠らない、気を抜かない
❻ I've let myself go a bit: 直訳的には「自分が若干くたびれるのを許してしまった」。
❼ I have to say: 言わせてもらえば
❽ be in much worse shape: ずっとひどい状態にある。shape は in good/bad shape などの形で「状態」「体調」の意になる。
❾ Compared with you: 君と比較するなら

ももう、こづき回されて黙っている男じゃなかったからな」

　私たちはふたたび、コテージにはさまれた狭い曲がりくねった街路を歩いていた。娘はまだ先を行っていたが、さっきよりずっと早足になっていた。前方の、どこかの角を彼女が曲がる姿を危うく見逃しかけることも何度かあって、よほど気をつけないと置いてけぼりを喰ってしまうと思った。

「もちろんいまの私は」とロジャー・バトンが言っているのが聞こえた。「いささかくたびれてしまっている。だがな君、君の方がずっとひどいと思うぜ。君と較べれば、私はスポーツ選手だ。ありていに言って、君は汚らしい老いぼれの浮浪者だ。そうだろう？　だけどね、君がいなくなってからも、長いあいだ私は君を偶像視しつづけたんだよ。フレッチャーはこんなことをするかな？　僕がこんなことしているのを見たらフレッチャーはどう思うだろう？　そうとも。それが15かそこらになって、やっと私も過去をふり返って、君の正体を見抜けるようになったのさ。もちろん、ものすごく腹が立っ

⑩ Not to put too fine a point on it: 直訳は「それについて過度に細かい（fine）ことを言うのでなければ」＝はっきり言えば

⑪ I looked back on it all and saw through you: すべてをふり返ってみて、君の正体を見抜いた。see through ...: ～を看破する、見抜く

very angry, of course. Even now, I still think about it sometimes. I look back and think, Well, he was just ❶a thoroughly nasty so-and-so. He had a little more weight and muscle at that age than I did, a little more ❷confidence, and he ❸took full advantage. Yes, it's very clear, looking back, what ❹a nasty little person you were. Of course, I'm not ❺implying ❻you still are today. We all change. ❼That much I'm willing to accept.'

'Have you been living here long?' I asked, wishing to ❽change the subject.

'Oh, seven years or so. Of course, they talk about you a lot around here. I sometimes tell them about ❾our early association. "But he won't remember me," I always tell them. "Why would he remember a ❿skinny little boy he used to bully and ⓫have at his beck and call?" Anyway, the young people here, they talk about you more and more these days. Certainly, the ones who've never seen you tend to idealize you the most. I suppose you've come

❶ a thoroughly nasty so-and-so: a so-and-so だけでも「嫌な奴」だが、さらに thoroughly nasty（とことんタチの悪い）が加わって相当な強調になっている。

❷ confidence: 自信

❸ took full advantage: 自分の有利な立場を全面的に利用した。相手の弱みにつけ込む、というニュアンスがこのフレーズにはたいてい伴う。

❹ a nasty little person: 実に嫌な奴。little はこのように、形容詞と名詞のあいだにはさまって、好悪の感情両方を強調しうる。*They live in a nice little cottage in the country.*（彼らは田舎のすてきな別荘に住んでいる。『ロングマン英和辞典』）

❺ imply(ing): 〜をほのめかす

❻ you still are: you still are a nasty little person

た。いまでも時おり考えるよ。あのころをふり返って、ああ、あいつはとことん嫌な野郎だったなあ、あのころは私より少しばかり体重と筋肉があって、少しばかり自信があったのをいいことに、それにとことんつけ込んだんだとね。そうとも、いまにして思えば火を見るより明らかだとも、君がどんなに鼻持ちならないクズ野郎だったか。もちろん、いまの君もそうだと言ってるんじゃないぜ。人はみんな変わる。それくらいは私としても認めるにやぶさかでない」

「この村にはもう長いのかい？」と私は、話題を変えたくて訊いた。

「ああ、7年くらいになる。もちろん、ここでは君はしじゅう話題になっている。私もときどき、子供のころ君とつき合いがあったことを連中に話したりする。『でも向こうは覚えちゃいないさ』といつも言うんだ。『昔いじめていた、顎で動かしてた痩せっぽちの子供のことなんか覚えてるはずがないさ』とね。まあとにかく、このへんの若い連中は、近頃ますます君のことを話題にするようになっている。少なくとも、君のことを一番偶像視するのは、君を全然見たことのない連中だよ。君もたぶん、そこにつけ込もうとして戻っ

❼ That much I'm willing to accept: そこまでは私も認める気がある
❽ change the subject: 話題を変える
❾ our early association: 私たちの、幼い頃の関係
❿ skinny: 痩せっぽちの
⓫ have at his beck and call: 意のままにあしらう

back to ❶capitalize on all that. Still, I shouldn't blame you. ❷You're entitled to try and ❸salvage a little self-respect.'

We suddenly found ourselves facing ❹an open field, and we both halted. Glancing back, I saw that we ❺had walked our way out of the village; the last of the cottages were some distance behind us. Just as I had feared, we had lost the young woman; in fact, I realised we had not been following her for some time.

At that moment, the moon emerged, and I saw we were standing at the edge of ❻a vast grassy field—❼extending, I supposed, far beyond what I could see by the moon.

Roger Button turned to me. His face in the moonlight seemed gentle, almost ❽affectionate.

'Still,' he said, 'it's time to forgive. You shouldn't keep worrying so much. As you see, certain things from the past will come back to you ❾in the end. ❿But then we can't ⓫be held accountable for what we did when we were very young.'

❶ to capitalize on all that: そういうもろもろにつけ込もうと
❷ You're entitled to ...: 君には〜する権利がある
❸ salvage a little self-respect: 少しの自尊心を救い出す
❹ an open field: 開けた野原
❺ had walked our way out of the village: 歩いているうちにいつしか村の外に出ていた
❻ a vast grassy field: 広大な、草深い原っぱ
❼ extending ... far beyond what I could see: 見える範囲よりずっと先までのびて
❽ affectionate: 愛情のこもった
❾ in the end: 最後には、いつかは
❿ But then: そうは言っても

てきたんだろうな。まあ無理もない。若干の自尊心を取り戻す権利は君にだってあるからな」

突然、開けた野原の前に出て、私たちは二人とも立ち止まった。チラッと背後をふり返ると、私たちはいつのまにか村の外に出てしまっていた。最後のコテージもいまではだいぶうしろに遠ざかっている。案の定、私たちは娘を見失ってしまった。実際、もうだいぶ前から自分たちが彼女について行っていなかったことに私は思いあたった。

その瞬間、月が出て、我々二人が広大な野原の端に立っているのがわかった。野原は月の光で見える範囲よりはるか向こうまで広がっているようだった。

ロジャー・バトンは私の方を向いた。月光に照らされたその顔は優しげで、ほとんど親愛の情すら感じられた。

「だがもう許すべき時だ」と彼は言った。「君もそんなに心配しなくていい。君にもわかっている通り、過去のある種の物事は、結局は自分自身にはね返ってくる。とはいえ、すごく若かったころにやったことの責任を負わされるわけにはいかないさ」

⓫ be held accountable for ...: 〜の責任を負わされる

'❶No doubt you're right,' I said. Then I turned and looked around in the darkness. 'But now I'm not sure where to go. You see, there were some young people waiting for me in their cottage. By now they'd have a warm fire ready for me and some hot tea. And some home-baked cakes, perhaps even a good stew. And the moment I entered, ❷ushered in by that young lady we were following just now, ❸they'd all have burst into applause. There'd be smiling, ❹adoring faces all around me. That's what's waiting for me somewhere. ❺Except I'm not sure where I should go.'

Roger Button ❻shrugged. 'Don't worry, you'll get there ❼easily enough. Except, you know, that girl ❽was being a little misleading if she implied you could walk to Wendy's cottage. It's much too far. You'd really need to catch a bus. Even then, it's quite a long journey. About two hours, I'd say. But don't worry, I'll show you where you can pick up your bus.'

With that, he began to walk back toward the cottages. As I

❶ No doubt you're right: p. 230, l. 8 の Have you been living here long? に較べれば少しは相手の話に合わせているが、ここでもすぐまた I turned and looked ... と、話し手の関心はあっさりよそを向いてしまう。
❷ ushered in by ...: ～に案内されて
❸ they'd all have burst into applause: みんな一気に拍手喝采しただろう
❹ adoring <adore: ～を崇める
❺ Except: ただし、ただ
❻ shrug(ged): 肩をすくめる。shrug については p. 158, l. 2 の註を参照。
❼ easily enough: それほど苦労せずに
❽ was being a little misleading: いささか誤解を招く言い方をした。was being ... については、p. 206, l. 4 の 'You're being unfair' の註を参照。

「まったくその通り」と私は言った。それから、向き直って、周りの暗闇を見渡した。「でもいま、私はどこへ行ったらいいかわからないんだ。いいかい、若い連中が何人か、コテージで私を待っていたんだ。もういまごろは、私のために暖炉も暖かく焚いて、熱いお茶を用意してくれているはずなんだ。それとホームメードのケーキに、ひょっとしたら美味しいシチューも。そして、ついさっきまで我々の前を歩いていたあのお嬢さんに連れられて私が入っていったとたん、みんないっせいに喝采したはずなんだ。私の周りじゅう、笑顔の、憧れと崇拝の念をみなぎらせた顔が輪になっていたはずなんだ。そういうのがどこかで私を待ってるはずなんだよ。でも私はどこへ行ったらいいかわからないんだ」

ロジャー・バトンは肩をすくめた。「心配するな、いずれ着く。わけないことさ。ただしだな、もしあの女の子が、ウェンディのコテージまで歩いていけるようなことを言ったとしたら、それはちょっと誤解を招く言い方だったな。歩くには全然遠すぎる。バスに乗るしかないよ。それでもずいぶん長旅だ、二時間というところかな。でも心配するな、バスが来るところまで連れていってやるから」

そう言って、ロジャー・バトンはコテージの並ぶ方に戻っていきはじめた。

followed, I could sense that the hour had got very late and my companion ❶was anxious to get some sleep. We spent several minutes walking around the cottages again, and then he brought us out into the village square. ❷In fact, it was so small and ❸shabby it hardly ❹merited being called a square; it was little more than ❺a patch of green beside a ❻solitary street lamp. Just visible beyond ❼the pool of light ❽cast by the lamp were a few shops, all shut up for the night. There was complete silence and nothing was stirring. ❾A light mist was ❿hovering over the ground.

Roger Button stopped before we had reached the green and pointed.

'There,' he said. 'If you stand there, a bus will ⓫come along. As I say, it's not a short journey. About two hours. But don't worry, I'm sure your young people will wait. They've so little else to believe in these days, you see.'

'It's very late,' I said. 'Are you sure a bus will come?'

❶ was anxious to ...: 〜したがっていた
❷ In fact: ここでは「村の広場といっても、実は〜」というふうに逆接的なつながりを作っている。
❸ shabby: みすぼらしい
❹ merit(ed): 〜に値する
❺ a patch of green: 緑の一画。patch は案外訳しづらいが、全体の中でそこだけ違って見える部分、という含みがつねにある。a bald patch:（ほかの部分は毛があるのに）そこだけ禿げた部分。
❻ solitary: ひとつだけぽつんとある
❼ the pool of light:「光の水たまり」という直訳でもいいかもしれない。
❽ cast by the lamp: 街灯によって投げかけられた
❾ A light mist: かすかなもや

そのうしろをついて行きながら、いまやもうすっかり遅い時間であり、彼がもう寝床に入りたがっていることを私は感じとった。何分かまたコテージのあいだを歩き回った末に、彼は私を村の広場に連れ出した。実のところそこはものすごく狭い、みすぼらしい場所で、およそ広場の名に値しなかった。猫の額程度の緑地が、ぽつんと一本立った街灯のかたわらにあるだけだ。街灯から降り注ぐ光のたまりのすぐ向こうに、何軒か商店がかすかに見えたが、もうどこも店仕舞いしていた。あたりはしんと静まり返り、何ひとつ動くものはない。薄いもやが地面の上に漂っていた。

我々が緑地に着くより先に、ロジャー・バトンは立ち止まって指さした。

「あそこだ」と彼は言った。「あそこに立っていれば、バスが来る。さっきも言った通り、短い距離じゃない。二時間くらいだ。でも心配は要らん、若い連中はきっと待ってくれるさ。今日、彼らにはほかに信じられるものなんてほとんどないからな」

「もうすごく遅い時間だけど、本当にバスは来るのかい？」と私は訊いた。

❿ hover(ing): 浮かぶ、漂う
⓫ come along: やって来る

'Oh, yes. Of course, you may have to wait. But ❶eventually a bus will come.' Then he touched me ❷reassuringly on the shoulder. 'I can see it might get a little lonely standing out here. But once the bus arrives ❸your spirits will rise, ❹believe me. Oh, yes. That bus is always a joy. It'll be ❺brightly lit up, and it's always full of cheerful people, laughing and joking and ❻pointing out the window. Once you ❼board it, you'll feel warm and comfortable, and the other passengers will chat with you, perhaps offer you things to eat or drink. There may even be singing— ❽that depends on the driver. Some drivers ❾encourage it, others don't. Well, Fletcher, it was good to see you.'

We shook hands, then he turned and walked away. I watched him disappear into the darkness between two cottages.

I walked up to the green and put my bag down at the foot of ❿the lamppost. I listened for the sound of ⓫a vehicle in the distance, but the night ⓬was utterly still. Nevertheless, I had been

❶ eventually: p. 194, l. 12と同様。
❷ reassuringly: 元気づけるように
❸ your spirits will rise: 元気も出てくるだろう
❹ believe me:「私を信じてくれ」ではなく「本当さ」という程度。
❺ brightly lit up: あかあかと照明が灯って
❻ pointing out the window: 窓の外を指さして
❼ board it: 乗車する
❽ that depends on the driver: それは運転手次第だ
❾ encourage: ～を奨励する
❿ the lamppost: 街灯柱
⓫ a vehicle: 乗り物、車
⓬ was utterly still: まったく静かだった

「ああ、来るとも。まあしばらく待たされるかもしれない。でもいずれは来るのさ」。そう言ってロジャー・バトンは、励ますように私の肩に触れた。「ここで立っていると、いくらか心細くなるかもしれない。それはわかる。でも、いったんバスが来たら、気持ちもいっぺんに明るくなるはずさ、本当だとも。そうとも。あのバスはいつ乗っても実に愉しい。こうこうと明かりがついていて、いつだって陽気な人たちで賑わっている。みんな笑って、冗談を言って、窓の外の景色を指さしてるんだ。乗ってしまえば、暖かい、心地よい気持ちになるはずだし、ほかの乗客たちが話しかけてきて、食べ物や飲み物も分けてくれたりする。歌だって歌うかもしれない――これは運転手次第だね。歌を奨励する運転手もいれば、しないのもいるんだ。それじゃフレッチャー、会えてよかったよ」

私たちは握手し、やがてロジャー・バトンは回れ右して、立ち去った。二軒のコテージのあいだの暗闇に彼が消えていくのを私は見守った。

私は緑地まで歩いていって、街灯の下に鞄を下ろした。遠くに乗り物の音が聞こえないかと耳を澄ませたが、夜はしんと静まり返っていた。にもかかわらず、ロジャー・バトンが聞かせてくれたバスの話のおかげで、私の気持

cheered by Roger Button's ❶description of the bus. Moreover, I thought of the reception ❷awaiting me at my journey's end—of the adoring faces of the young people—and felt ❸the stirrings of optimism somewhere deep within me.

❶ description: 描写、説明
❷ await(ing): ～を待つ
❸ the stirrings of optimism: 楽天のうごめき

ちは明るくなっていた。それに、旅の終わりに待っている歓迎のことを想い、憧れ、崇める若い人たちの顔を想うと、自分のなかのどこか奥深いところで楽天が息づくのが感じられた。

ちなみに

2007年6月にイシグロ氏をインタビューしたときに聞いたのだが、この作品はそもそも長篇 *The Unconsoled* (1995) の下準備として書いたもので、短篇として発表する気はなかったという（たしかに、「バス」というモチーフをはじめ、この作品には大長篇 *The Unconsoled* を彷彿とさせる要素がいくつもある)。ところが、フランスの出版社から読者プレゼントの小冊子用の作品を、と求められて仕方なくこれを送ったところ、勝手に *The New Yorker* にも送られて、本人のあずかり知らぬところで掲載が決まったという。下準備がこのレベルなのだとしたら、ほかにいったいどれだけの高水準の作品が発表されずに眠っているのか……。

The Miner

James Robertson

坑夫

ジェームズ・ロバートソン

★☆☆

ジェームズ・ロバートソン
(James Robertson, 1958-)

現代スコットランドを代表する作家の一人。20 世紀後半のスコットランドの歴史を丸ごと捉えた大作 *And the Land Lay Still* をはじめとする長篇 6 作のほか、短篇集、詩集、児童書など著作多数、出版社も経営している。本作 'The Miner' は *365: Stories* (2014) から。

All the stories in the world originally came from one source, ❶a mine in a remote and ❷desolate place where only ❸the story-miners lived. ❹The stories came in many shapes and sizes—some heavy and ❺bulky, some smooth and ❻delicate, others sharp and ❼awkward to hold—but they had one common ❽property: something in each one shone, or ❾glittered, reflecting light ❿in its own special way.

The stories were ⓫dispatched, ⓬unrefined, across the world, to people who had no knowledge of the mine's existence. When they ⓭came across one of the stories ⓮in their own locality, they ⓯assumed that it belonged to them.

Over many centuries the mine ⓰workings grew deeper and more complex. When one ⓱seam was ⓲exhausted, another was opened. Still, it ⓳became increasingly difficult to find and ⓴extract new stories. ㉑As this happened, the miners themselves grew fewer.

❶ a mine: 鉱山
❷ desolate: 荒涼とした
❸ the story-miners: たとえば goldminers なら「金山労働者たち」。
❹ The stories came in many shapes and sizes: この come in はたとえば The watch comes in two sizes(この腕時計は2サイズあります)などと同じ。
❺ bulky: かさのある、大きく扱いにくい
❻ delicate: 優美な、壊れやすい
❼ awkward to hold: 持ちづらい
❽ (a) property: 特徴
❾ glitter(ed): すぐ前の shone (<shine) に較べて、同じ「光る」でもキラキラ・ギラギラ感が強い。
❿ in its own special way: それ独自のやり方で
⓫ dispatch(ed): ～を発送する

世界中の物語はすべて、元はひとつの源から出てきていた。その源とは、物語坑夫たちしか住まない、人里離れた荒涼たる場所にある鉱山である。物語たちはいろんな形や大きさで採(と)れる。重くてかさばるのもあれば、滑らかで華奢なのもあり、ぎざぎざで持ちづらいのもある。だがひとつだけ、共通の特徴がある。一つひとつの中の何かが、それぞれ独自のやり方で光を反射し、きらめくのだ。

物語は精練されないまま世界各地、そんな鉱山の存在などつゆ知らぬ人々のもとへ送り出された。自分の地元でそうした物語に出会った人々は、それが元から自分たちのものだったと信じて疑わなかった。

何世紀にもわたって、鉱山の坑道はどんどん深く、複雑になっていった。ひとつの鉱脈が掘り尽くされると、別の鉱脈が拓かれた。それでも、新しい物語を見つけて採掘するのはますます困難になっていった。それとともに、坑夫の数も減っていった。上の世代は死に絶えた。若い家族はもっと楽で実

⓬ unrefined: 精錬されないまま。stories は一貫して、あたかも鉱物のように語られている。
⓭ came across >come across ...: 〜に出会う
⓮ in their own locality: 地元で
⓯ assume(d): 当然〜だと考える
⓰ working(s): 採掘場、坑道
⓱ (a) seam: 鉱脈
⓲ exhaust(ed): 〜を使い果たす
⓳ became increasingly difficult: だんだん難しくなっていった
⓴ extract: 〜を採掘する
㉑ As this happened: こういうことが起きるとともに

The older generation died. Younger families left, seeking ❶ less demanding and more rewarding work. ❷A time came when only one miner remained—a strong and skilful labourer, but the last of his kind. One day he came up from the mine ❸empty-handed: there were no more stories down there.

❹Sad though he was to see the end of a long tradition, the miner was a ❺realistic man. He collected his tools and ❻personal belongings, and ❼set off in search of a new occupation.

How long he walked is not recorded, but ❽eventually he ❾left behind the ❿bleak landscape familiar to him, and travelled through a country of thick forests, green meadows, ⓫rushing rivers and ⓬cultivated fields. He passed through villages and towns and spent time in huge cities. And he began to notice—lying at the roadside, or ⓭marking the edges of flowerbeds in parks and gardens, or ⓮abandoned in heaps in ⓯disused warehouses—the same ⓰multiform stories that he had once ⓱mined. He collected

❶ less demanding and more rewarding work: これほどきつくなく、もっと実入りのいい仕事。rewarding は文脈によっては「やりがいのある」の意味にもなりうるが、ここでは単に収入がいい、ということ。
❷ A time came when ...: やがて〜する時が来た
❸ empty-handed: 手ぶらで、何の収穫もなく
❹ Sad though he was: though he was sad
❺ realistic: 現実的な
❻ personal belongings: 持ち物
❼ set off: 出発した
❽ eventually: やがて。p. 194, l. 12 の註を参照。
❾ left behind ...: 〜をあとにした
❿ bleak: 荒涼とした

入りのいい仕事を求めて去っていった。とうとう、残った坑夫は一人だけになってしまった。逞しい、腕のいい職人ではあるが、もうこれが最後の一人だった。ある日彼は、何の収穫もなく坑道から上がってきた。もうそこには、ひとつの物語もなかったのだ。

長い伝統が終わるのを見るのは悲しかったが、坑夫は現実的な人間であった。仕事の道具と、個人的な持ち物をまとめて、新しい職を求めて旅立った。

坑夫がどれくらい長く歩いたかは記録に残っていないが、見慣れた荒涼たる風景を後にした彼は、鬱蒼と木の茂る森、緑の草原、勢いよく流れる川、耕された畑の只中を旅していった。村や町を抜け、巨大な都市でしばし時を過ごした。そして彼は気づきはじめた――自分がかつて採掘した種々の物語が、道端に転がっていたり、公園や庭園の花壇を縁どっていたり、使われなくなった倉庫に放置され山と積まれていたりするのを。それら捨てられた物

⓫ rushing rivers: 奔流の川
⓬ cultivated fields: 耕作された畑
⓭ marking the edges of flowerbeds: 花壇の縁を成して
⓮ abandoned in heaps: 捨てられて山になって
⓯ disused warehouses: 使われなくなった倉庫
⓰ multiform: 多様な、さまざまな
⓱ mine(d): ～を採掘する

several of the ❶discarded ones, and used his tools to ❷recut or polish them a little. Then he walked on, ❸discreetly depositing them in pubs, churches, schools, theatres, places of work, places of play . . .

And when people came across one of these ❹slightly altered stories, they picked it up and took it home, assuming that it belonged to them.

❶ discarded: 捨てられた
❷ recut: ～を再切断する
❸ discreetly depositing them: それらをそっと置いて
❹ slightly altered: わずかに変えられた

語のうちいくつかを彼は拾い集めて、道具を使って切ったり、若干磨いたりしてから、あちこちにさりげなく置いていった。パブ、教会、学校、劇場、職場、遊び場……。

これらわずかに変更を加えられた物語に出会うと、人々はそれを拾って、元から自分のものだったと信じて疑わず家に持って帰った。

ちなみに

この 'The Miner' を収めた短篇集 *365* には、文字どおり 365 本の短篇が収められている。作者ロバートソンはこれら 365 本の小品を、2013 年の 1 月 1 日から 12 月 31 日にかけて、一日一本ずつ書いていった。したがって作品にはすべて日付がついている。この 'The Miner' は（勘のいい読者はもうおわかりだろうが）12 月 31 日の作品である。

365 というタイトルにはもうひとつ意味がある。収録された 365 本の作品はすべて、それぞれ 365 語から成っているのである。

授業後の雑談

7作品精読、お疲れさま。各作品について、雑談的に補足しておきます。

I. A. Ireland, "Ending for a Ghost Story" は、作品のあとに添えた〈ちなみに〉にも書いたとおり、おそらくはボルヘスたちの捏造ですが、2008年に出た *A Companion to the British and Irish Story* というれっきとした文学史の本（edited by Cheryl Alexander Malcolm and David Malcom, Wiley-Blackwell, 2008）の "The British and Irish Ghost Story and Tale of the Supernatural" という章には I. A. Ireland に関する記述が載っていて、ボルヘスらがこの著者の主著として挙げている *A Brief History of Nightmare* についても具体的に解説しています。とはいえ、ボルヘスたちが提供した以上の資料を参照した痕跡はいっさいありません。ひょっとすると、執筆者（Becky DiBiasio という学者です）がボルヘスたちの遊戯的捏造の精神を引き継いで、真面目な文学史のなかにさらなる捏造を忍び込ませたのか……。

ごく短いながら、"Ending for a Ghost Story" は性差を考える上でも有効な物語に思えます。登場人物の男と女を入れたら、全然違う話になります。なぜそうなるのか？　という問いから話はいろんな方向に広がりそうです。

W. W. Jacobs, "The Monkey's Paw" はもう何度も何度も映画化・ドラマ化等々されているので、すでに触れていた方も多いのではないでしょうか。僕も小学生か中学生のころテレビでドラマを見た覚えがあります。夫が三度目に猿の手を持ち上げる瞬間は、いまも目に浮かびます。

第2巻に登場するアメリカの作家スチュアート・ダイベックが書いた "Ant" という短篇には、"The Monkey's Paw" が印象的な形で出てきます。戦争から帰ってきた、明らかに PSTD（心的外傷後ストレス障害）を抱えている叔父さんが、甥っ子と物語ごっこをする。そのレパートリーのひとつが "The Monkey's Paw" なのです。"Ant" はウェブにも上がっているので（http://coopercrw.blogspot.com/2005/02/ant-by-stuart-dybek.html）、よかったら読んでみてください。

Shirley Jackson は、じわじわ効いてくる怪奇小説の名手であり、しかも英語は 20 世紀なかばの飾らないアメリカ英語なので、語学的にも割合敷居は低いと思います。その手のものが好きな方は手に取ってみてください。本書で取り上げた "The Lottery" を表題作にした短篇集が出ているし（*The Lottery and Other Stories*）、また、その短篇集に加え、長篇 2 本などを一冊に収めた版が、アメリカ文学に関しもっとも信頼できるシリーズ The Library of America に入っています（Shirley Jackson, *Novels and Stories*）。長篇では *The Haunting of Hill House* の、何が起きているのかよくわからないまま怖さが伝わってくる感じが素晴らしいです（これも The Library of America 版に入っています）。

"The Ones Who Walk Away from Omelas" の作者 Ursula K. Le Guin は、「ゲド戦記」をはじめ多くの邦訳が出ているので、すでに大半の方がご存じでしょう。お気づきの方も多いと思いますが、"The Ones Who Walk Away from Omelas" というこの物語、ある意味ですぐ前の "The Lottery" とほとんど同じ話だと言えます。共同体の幸福が、一人の人間の犠牲の上になり立つとしたら……。二作がどう同じでどう違うか、考えてみても面白いかと思います。〈ちなみに〉でも書いたとおり、ル＝グウィンはウィリアム・ジェームズの哲学論文の一節に刺激されてこの作品を書いたと述べていて、さらに、書いたあと人から「『カラマーゾフの兄弟』のイヴァンも同じこと言ってるよね」と指摘されてああそうだったと気づいた、とも述べています。そう考えると、ドストエフスキーがル＝グウィンを経由してシャーリイ・ジャクスンにまでつながって行きます。

William Burroughs, "The Junky's Christmas" は 1989 年に発表されたクリスマス・ストーリーです。クリスマス・ストーリーというと Charles Dickens, *Christmas Carol*（1843）や O. Henry, "The Gift of the Magi"（1905）など、19 世紀から 20 世紀初頭のものが中心ですが、これは現代の古典になってもおかしくない愛すべき作品だと思います。

もうひとつ、愛すべき現代のクリスマス・ストーリーというと、"The Junky's Christmas" の翌年のクリスマス当日に *The New York Times* に掲載された、Paul Auster, "Auggie Wrens Christmas Story"（1990）があります。これはウェブ上では読めませんが、NPR（National Public Radio）で作者本人の煙草喫いすぎ声で朗読を聴くことはできます：https://www.npr.org/templates/story/story.php?storyId=4244994（あるいは NPR のホー

ム npr.org に行って Auggie Wren をサーチ)。

Kazuo Ishiguro も英語は比較的易しく、作品はどれも小説として見事なので、何か長篇を英語で読みとおしたいのだが、と相談されると僕は彼の *The Remains of the Day*（1989）や *Never Let Me Go*（2005）を薦めることが多いです。が、イシグロ作品の中でも強烈な印象を残す異色作を求めるなら、何と言ってもこの "A Village After Dark" が青写真の役割を果たしたという *The Unconsoled*（1995）です。長大で、読んでいてしんどい部分もところどころありますが、長い長い夢にずっとうなされている（いた）かのような読中・読後感は圧倒的です。この短篇を読んだあとに読めば、なるほど短篇のあのシーンをこうやって膨らませたわけか、といったこともわかるというボーナスがあります。

「物語を楽しむ」の巻は、やはり物語をめぐる物語で締めくくりたい。James Robertson, "The Miner" は、365 語で書かれた短篇 365 本を収めた短篇集 *365*（2014）の最後にもぴったりでしたが、この巻の締めくくりにもうってつけではないかと思います。ちなみにウェブ上には、ロバートソンがこの 365 本をすべて朗読し、フィドル奏者 Aidan O'Rourke が音楽をつけたサイト *365: Stories + Music* があります（https://three-six-five.net/Stories-And-Music)。作者によるスコットランド訛りの味わい深い朗読が聴けます。

2021 年 3 月

柴田　元幸

編集協力
高橋由香理・滝野沢友理・福間恵・今井亮一・青木比登美

組版・レイアウト
古正佳緒里・山本太平

社内協力
三谷裕・望月羔子・高見沢紀子・三島知子・鈴木美和・松本千晶・星野龍

編訳註者

柴田元幸（しばた もとゆき）

翻訳家、東京大学名誉教授。東京都生まれ。ポール・オースター、レベッカ・ブラウン、スティーヴン・ミルハウザー、スチュアート・ダイベック、スティーヴ・エリクソンなど、現代アメリカ文学を数多く翻訳。2010 年、トマス・ピンチョン『メイスン＆ディクスン』（新潮社）で日本翻訳文化賞を受賞。翻訳に、マーク・トウェイン『ハックルベリー・フィンの冒けん』（研究社）『トム・ソーヤーの冒険』（新潮文庫）、ジョゼフ・コンラッド『ロード・ジム』（河出文庫）、エリック・マコーマック『雲』（東京創元社）、スティーヴン・ミルハウザー『ホーム・ラン』（白水社）など多数。編訳書に、『「ハックルベリー・フィンの冒けん」をめぐる冒けん』、レアード・ハント『英文創作教室　Writing Your Own Stories』（研究社）など。文芸誌『MONKEY』、および英語文芸誌 MONKEY 責任編集。2017 年、早稲田大学坪内逍遙大賞を受賞。

英文精読教室(えいぶんせいどくきょうしつ)
第1巻(だいかん)
物語(ものがたり)を楽(たの)しむ

● 2021年4月30日　初版発行 ●
● 2024年3月29日　4刷発行 ●

● 編訳註者 ●
柴田元幸(しばたもとゆき)

発行者 ● 吉田尚志

発行所 ● 株式会社　研究社

〒102-8152　東京都千代田区富士見 2-11-3

電話　営業 03-3288-7777（代）　編集 03-3288-7711（代）

振替　00150-9-26710

https://www.kenkyusha.co.jp/

KENKYUSHA

装丁 ● 久保和正

組版・レイアウト ● 渾天堂

印刷所 ● 図書印刷株式会社

ISBN 978-4-327-09901-5 C1082　Printed in Japan